The Caretaker
and
The Dumb Waiter

THE CARETAKER
and
THE DUMB WAITER

Two plays by
Harold Pinter

GROVE PRESS, INC.   NEW YORK

To Vivien

The Caretaker

This play was first presented by the Arts Theatre Club in association with Michael Codron and David Hall at the Arts Theatre, London WC 2, on 27th April, 1960.

On 30th May, 1960, the play was presented by Michael Codron and David Hall at the Duchess Theatre, London, with the following cast:

MICK, *a man in his late twenties*	Alan Bates
ASTON, *a man in his early thirties*	Peter Woodthorpe
DAVIES, *an old man*	Donald Pleasence

The play was directed by Donald McWhinnie

The action of the play takes place in a house in west London.

ACT I A night in winter
ACT II A few seconds later
ACT III A fortnight later

PHOTOGRAPHIC INSERT

Photos from the American production by
Sam Siegel

A room. A window in the back wall, the bottom half covered by a sack. An iron bed along the left wall. Above it a small cupboard, paint buckets, boxes containing nuts, screws, etc. More boxes, vases, by the side of the bed. A door, up right. To the right of the window, a mound: a kitchen sink, a step-ladder, a coal bucket, a lawn-mower, a shopping trolley, boxes, sideboard drawers. Under this mound an iron bed. In front of it a gas stove. On the gas stove a statue of Buddha. Down right, a fireplace. Around it a couple of suitcases, a rolled carpet, a blow-lamp, a wooden chair on its side, boxes, a number of ornaments, a clothes horse, a few short planks of wood, a small electric fire and a very old electric toaster. Below this a pile of old newspapers. Under ASTON'S *bed by the left wall, is an electrolux, which is not seen till used. A bucket hangs from the ceiling.*

Act One

MICK *is alone in the room, sitting on the bed. He wears a leather jacket.*

Silence.

He slowly looks about the room looking at each object in turn. He looks up at the ceiling, and stares at the bucket. Ceasing, he sits quite still, expressionless, looking out front.

Silence for thirty seconds.

A door bangs. Muffled voices are heard.

MICK *turns his head. He stands, moves silently to the door, goes out, and closes the door quietly.*

Silence.

Voices are heard again. They draw nearer, and stop. The door opens. ASTON *and* DAVIES *enter,* ASTON *first,* DAVIES *following, shambling, breathing heavily.*

ASTON *wears an old tweed overcoat, and under it a thin shabby dark-blue pinstripe suit, single-breasted, with a pullover and faded shirt and tie.* DAVIES *wears a worn brown overcoat, shapeless trousers, a waistcoat, vest, no shirt, and sandals.* ASTON *puts the key in his pocket and closes the door.* DAVIES *looks about the room.*

ASTON. Sit down.
DAVIES. Thanks. (*Looking about.*) Uuh. . . .
ASTON. Just a minute.

> ASTON *looks around for a chair, sees one lying on its side by the rolled carpet at the fireplace, and starts to get it out.*

DAVIES. Sit down? Huh . . . I haven't had a good sit down . . . I haven't had a proper sit down . . . well, I couldn't tell you. . . .

ASTON (*placing the chair*). Here you are.

DAVIES. Ten minutes off for tea-break in the middle of the night in that place and I couldn't find a seat, not one. All them Greeks had it, Poles, Greeks, Blacks, the lot of them, all them aliens had it. And they had me working there . . . they had me working. . . .

> ASTON *sits on the bed, takes out a tobacco tin and papers, and begins to roll himself a cigarette.* DAVIES *watches him.*

All them Blacks had it, Blacks, Greeks, Poles, the lot of them, that's what, doing me out of a seat, treating me like dirt. When he come at me tonight I told him.

> *Pause.*

ASTON. Take a seat.

DAVIES. Yes, but what I got to do first, you see, what I got to do, I got to loosen myself up, you see what I mean? I could have got done in down there.

> DAVIES *exclaims loudly, punches downward with closed fist, turns his back to* ASTON *and stares at the wall.*
> *Pause.* ASTON *lights a cigarette.*

ASTON. You want to roll yourself one of these?

DAVIES (*turning*). What? No, no, I never smoke a cigarette. (*Pause. He comes forward.*) I'll tell you what, though. I'll have a bit of that tobacco there for my pipe, if you like.

ASTON (*handing him the tin*). Yes. Go on. Take some out of that.

DAVIES. That's kind of you, mister. Just enough to fill my pipe, that's all. (*He takes a pipe from his pocket and fills it.*) I had a tin, only . . . only a while ago. But it was knocked off. It was knocked off on the Great West Road. (*He holds out the tin.*) Where shall I put it?

ASTON. I'll take it.

DAVIES (*handing the tin*). When he comes at me tonight I told him. Didn't I? You heard me tell him, didn't you?

ASTON. I saw him have a go at you.

DAVIES. Go at me? You wouldn't grumble. The filthy skate an old man like me, I've had dinner with the best.

Pause.

ASTON. Yes, I saw him have a go at you.

DAVIES. All them toe-rags, mate, got the manners of pigs. I might have been on the road a few years but you can take it from me I'm clean. I keep myself up. That's why I left my wife. Fortnight after I married her, no, not so much as that, no more than a week, I took the lid off a saucepan, you know what was in it? A pile of her underclothing, unwashed. The pan for vegetables, it was. The vegetable pan. That's when I left her and I haven't seen her since.

DAVIES *turns, shambles across the room, comes face to face with a statue of Buddha standing on the gas stove, looks at it and turns.*

I've eaten my dinner off the best of plates. But I'm not young any more. I remember the days I was as handy as any of them. They didn't take any liberties with me. But I haven't been so well lately. I've had a few attacks.

Pause.

(*Coming closer.*) Did you see what happened with that one?

ASTON. I only got the end of it.

DAVIES. Comes up to me, parks a bucket of rubbish at me tells me to take it out the back. It's not my job to take out the, bucket! They got a boy there for taking out the bucket. I wasn't engaged to take out buckets. My job's cleaning the floor, clearing up the tables, doing a bit of washing-up, nothing to do with taking out buckets!

ASTON. Uh.

He crosses down right, to get the electric toaster.

DAVIES (*following*) Yes, well say I had! Even if I had! Even if I was supposed to take out the bucket, who was this git to come up and give me orders? We got the same standing. He's not my boss. He's nothing superior to me.

ASTON. What was he, a Greek?

DAVIES. Not him, he was a Scotch. He was a Scotchman. (ASTON *goes back to his bed with the toaster and starts to unscrew the plug.* DAVIES *follows him.*) You got an eye of him, did you?

ASTON. Yes.

DAVIES. I told him what to do with his bucket. Didn't I? You heard. Look here, I said, I'm an old man, I said, where I was brought up we had some idea how to talk to old people with the proper respect, we was brought up with the right ideas, if I had a few years off me I'd . . . I'd break you in half. That was after the guvnor give me the bullet. Making too much commotion, he says. Commotion, me! Look here, I said to him, I got my rights. I told him that. I might have been on the road but nobody's got more rights than I have. Let's have a bit of fair play, I said. Anyway, he give me the bullet. (*He sits in the chair.*) That's the sort of place.

Pause.

If you hadn't come out and stopped that Scotch git I'd be inside the hospital now. I'd have cracked my head on that pavement if he'd have landed. I'll get him. One night I'll get him. When I find myself around that direction.

ASTON *crosses to the plug box to get another plug.*

I wouldn't mind so much but I left all my belongings in that place, in the back room there. All of them, the lot there was, you see, in this bag. Every lousy blasted bit of all my bleeding belongings I left down there now. In the rush of it. I bet he's having a poke around in it now this very moment.

ASTON. I'll pop down sometime and pick them up for you.

ASTON *goes back to his bed and starts to fix the plug on the toaster.*

DAVIES. Anyway, I'm obliged to you, letting me . . . letting me have a bit of a rest, like . . . for a few minutes. (*He looks about.*) This your room ?

ASTON. Yes.

DAVIES. You got a good bit of stuff here.

ASTON. Yes.

DAVIES. Must be worth a few bob, this . . . put it all together.

    Pause.

There's enough of it.

ASTON. There's a good bit of it, all right.

DAVIES. You sleep here, do you ?

ASTON. Yes.

DAVIES. What, in that ?

ASTON. Yes.

DAVIES. Yes, well, you'd be well out of the draught there.

ASTON. You don't get much wind.

DAVIES. You'd be well out of it. It's different when you're kipping out.

ASTON. Would be.

DAVIES. Nothing but wind then.

    Pause.

ASTON. Yes, when the wind gets up it. . . .

    Pause.

DAVIES. Yes. . . .

ASTON. Mmnn. . . .

    Pause.

DAVIES. Gets very draughty.

ASTON. Ah.

DAVIES. I'm very sensitive to it.

ASTON. Are you ?

DAVIES. Always have been.

    Pause.

You got more rooms then, have you ?

ASTON. Where?

DAVIES. I mean, along the landing here . . . up the landing there.

ASTON. They're out of commission.

DAVIES. Get away.

ASTON. They need a lot of doing to.

Slight pause.

DAVIES. What about downstairs?

ASTON. That's closed up. Needs seeing to. . . . The floors. . . .

Pause.

DAVIES. I was lucky you come into that caff. I might have been done by that Scotch git. I been left for dead more than once.

Pause.

I noticed that there was someone was living in the house next door.

ASTON. What?

DAVIES (*gesturing*). I noticed. . . .

ASTON. Yes. There's people living all along the road.

DAVIES. Yes, I noticed the curtains pulled down there next door as we come along.

ASTON. They're neighbours.

Pause.

DAVIES. This your house then, is it?

Pause.

ASTON. I'm in charge.

DAVIES. You the landlord, are you?

He puts a pipe in his mouth and puffs without lighting it.

Yes, I noticed them heavy curtains pulled across next door as we come along. I noticed them heavy big curtains right across the window down there. I thought there must be someone living there.

ASTON. Family of Indians live there.

DAVIES. Blacks?

ASTON. I don't see much of them.

DAVIES. Blacks, eh? (DAVIES *stands and moves about.*) Well you've got some knick-knacks here all right, I'll say that. I don't like a bare room. (ASTON *joins* DAVIES *upstage centre*). I'll tell you what, mate, you haven't got a spare pair of shoes?

ASTON. Shoes?

> ASTON *moves downstage right.*

DAVIES. Them bastards at the monastery let me down again.

ASTON (*going to his bed*). Where?

DAVIES. Down in Luton. Monastery down at Luton. . . . I got a mate at Shepherd's Bush, you see. . . .

ASTON (*looking under his bed*). I might have a pair.

DAVIES. I got this mate at Shepherd's Bush. In the convenience. Well, he was in the convenience. Run about the best convenience they had. (*He watches* ASTON.) Run about the best one. Always slipped me a bit of soap, any time I went in there. Very good soap. They have to have the best soap. I was never without a piece of soap, whenever I happened to be knocking about the Shepherd's Bush area.

ASTON (*emerging from under the bed with shoes*). Pair of brown.

DAVIES. He's gone now. Went. He was the one who put me on to this monastery. Just the other side of Luton. He'd heard they give away shoes.

ASTON. You've got to have a good pair of shoes.

DAVIES. Shoes? It's life and death to me. I had to go all the way to Luton in these.

ASTON. What happened when you got there, then?

> *Pause.*

DAVIES. I used to know a bootmaker in Acton. He was a good mate to me.

Pause.

You know what that bastard monk said to me?

Pause.

How many more Blacks you got around here then?

ASTON. What?

DAVIES. You got any more Blacks around here?

ASTON (*holding out the shoes*). See if these are any good.

DAVIES. You know what that bastard monk said to me? (*He looks over to the shoes.*) I think those'd be a bit small.

ASTON. Would they?

DAVIES. No, don't look the right size.

ASTON. Not bad trim.

DAVIES. Can't wear shoes that don't fit. Nothing worse. I said to this monk, here, I said, look here, mister, he opened the door, big door, he opened it, look here, mister, I said, I come all the way down here, look, I said, I showed him these, I said, you haven't got a pair of shoes, have you, a pair of shoes, I said, enough to keep me on my way. Look at these, they're nearly out, I said, they're no good to me. I heard you got a stock of shoes here. Piss off, he said to me. Now look here, I said, I'm an old man, you can't talk to me like that, I don't care who you are. If you don't piss off, he says, I'll kick you all the way to the gate. Now look here, I said, now wait a minute, all I'm asking for is a pair of shoes, you don't want to start taking liberties with me, it's taken me three days to get out here, I said to him, three days without a bite, I'm worth a bite to eat, en I? Get out round the corner to the kitchen, he says, get out round the corner, and when you've had your meal, piss off out of it. I went round to this kitchen, see? Meal they give me! A bird, I tell you, a little bird, a little tiny bird, he could have ate it in under two minutes. Right, they said to me, you've had your meal, get off out of it. Meal? I said, what do you think I am, a dog? Nothing better than a dog. What do you think I am, a wild animal? What about them shoes I come all the way here to get I heard you was giving away ? I've a good mind to report you to your mother superior. One of them, an Irish hooligan, come at me. I cleared out. I took a short cut to Watford and picked up a pair there. Got onto the North Circular, just past Hendon, the sole come off, right where I was walking. Lucky I had my old ones wrapped up, still carrying them, otherwise I'd have been finished, man. So I've had to stay with these, you see, they're gone, they're no good, all the good's gone out of them.

ASTON. Try these.

> DAVIES *takes the shoes, takes off his sandals and tries them on.*

DAVIES. Not a bad pair of shoes. (*He trudges round the room.*) They're strong, all right. Yes. Not a bad shape of shoe. This leather's hardy, en't ? Very hardy. Some bloke tried to flog me some suede the other day. I wouldn't wear them. Can't beat leather, for wear. Suede goes off, it creases, it stains for life in five minutes. You can't beat leather. Yes. Good shoe this.

ASTON. Good.

> DAVIES *waggles his feet.*

DAVIES. Don't fit though.

ASTON. Oh ?

DAVIES. No. I got a very broad foot.

ASTON. Mmnn.

DAVIES. These are too pointed, you see.

ASTON. Ah.

DAVIES. They'd cripple me in a week. I mean these ones I got on, they're no good but at least they're comfortable. Not much cop, but I mean they don't hurt. (*He takes them off and gives them back.*) Thanks anyway, mister.

ASTON. I'll see what I can look out for you.

DAVIES. Good luck. I can't go on like this. Can't get from one place to another. And I'll have to be moving about, you see, try to get fixed up.

ASTON. Where you going to go?

DAVIES. Oh, I got one or two things in mind. I'm waiting for
the weather to break.

> *Pause.*

ASTON (*attending to the toaster*). Would . . . would you like
to sleep here?

DAVIES. Here?

ASTON. You can sleep here if you like.

DAVIES. Here? Oh, I don't know about that.

> *Pause.*

How long for?

ASTON. Till you . . . get yourself fixed up.

DAVIES (*sitting*). Ay well, that. . . .

ASTON. Get yourself sorted out. . . .

DAVIES. Oh, I'll be fixed up . . . pretty soon now. . . .

> *Pause.*

Where would I sleep?

ASTON. Here. The other rooms would . . . would be no
good to you.

DAVIES (*rising, looking about*). Here? Where?

ASTON (*rising, pointing upstage right*). There's a bed behind all
that.

DAVIES. Oh, I see. Well, that's handy. Well, that's . . . I tell
you what, I might do that . . . just till I get myself sorted
out. You got enough furniture here.

ASTON. I picked it up. Just keeping it here for the time being.
Thought it might come in handy.

DAVIES. This gas stove work, do it?

ASTON. No.

DAVIES. What do you do for a cup of tea?

ASTON. Nothing.

DAVIES. That's a bit rough. (DAVIES *observes the planks*.) You
building something?

ASTON. I might build a shed out the back.

DAVIES. Carpenter, eh? (*He turns to the lawn-mower.*) Got a
lawn?

ASTON. Have a look.

ASTON *lifts the sack at the window. They look out.*

DAVIES. Looks a bit thick.

ASTON. Overgrown.

DAVIES. What's that, a pond?

ASTON. Yes.

DAVIES. What you got, fish?

ASTON. No. There isn't anything in there.

Pause.

DAVIES. Where you going to put your shed?

ASTON (*turning*). I'll have to clear the garden first.

DAVIES. You'd need a tractor, man.

ASTON. I'll get it done.

DAVIES. Carpentry, eh?

ASTON (*standing still*). I like . . . working with my hands.

DAVIES *picks up the statue of Buddha.*

DAVIES. What's this?

ASTON (*taking and studying it*). That's a Buddha.

DAVIES. Get on.

ASTON. Yes. I quite like it. Picked it up in a . . . in a shop.
Looked quite nice to me. Don't know why. What do you
think of these Buddhas?

DAVIES. Oh, they're . . . they're all right, en't they?

ASTON. Yes, I was pleased when I got hold of this one. It's
very well made.

DAVIES *turns and peers under the sink, etc.*

DAVIES. This the bed here, is it?

ASTON (*moving to the bed*). We'll get rid of all that. The
ladder'll fit under the bed. (*They put the ladder under the bed.*)

DAVIES (*indicating the sink*). What about this?

ASTON. I think that'll fit in under here as well.

DAVIES. I'll give you a hand. (*They lift it.*) It's a ton weight, en't?

ASTON. Under here.

DAVIES. This in use at all, then?

ASTON. No. I'll be getting rid of it. Here.

> *They place the sink under the bed.*

There's a lavatory down the landing. It's got a sink in there. We can put this stuff over there.

> *They begin to move the coal bucket, shopping trolley, lawn-mower and sideboard drawers to the right wall.*

DAVIES (*stopping*). You don't share it, do you?

ASTON. What?

DAVIES. I mean you don't share the toilet with them Blacks, do you?

ASTON. They live next door.

DAVIES. They don't come in?

> ASTON *puts a drawer against the wall.*

Because, you know . . . I mean . . . fair's fair. . . .

> ASTON *goes to the bed, blows dust and shakes a blanket.*

ASTON. You see a blue case?

DAVIES. Blue case? Down here. Look. By the carpet.

> ASTON *goes to the case, opens it, takes out a sheet and pillow and puts them on the bed.*

That's a nice sheet.

ASTON. The blanket'll be a bit dusty.

DAVIES. Don't you worry about that.

> ASTON *stands upright, takes out his tobacco and begins to roll a cigarette. He goes to his bed and sits.*

ASTON. How are you off for money?

DAVIES. Oh well . . . now, mister, if you want the truth . . . I'm a bit short.

ASTON *takes some coins from his pocket, sorts them, and holds out five shillings.*

ASTON. Here's a few bob.

DAVIES (*taking the coins*). Thank you, thank you, good luck. I just happen to find myself a bit short. You see, I got nothing for all that week's work I did last week. That's the position, that's what it is.

Pause.

ASTON. I went into a pub the other day. Ordered a Guinness. They gave it to me in a thick mug. I sat down but I couldn't drink it. I can't drink Guinness from a thick mug. I only like it out of a tin glass. I had a few sips but I couldn't finish it.

ASTON *picks up a screwdriver and plug from the bed and begins to poke the plug.*

DAVIES (*with great feeling*). If only the weather would break! Then I'd be able to get down to Sidcup!

ASTON. Sidcup?

DAVIES. The weather's so blasted bloody awful, how can I get down to Sidcup in these shoes?

ASTON. Why do you want to get down to Sidcup?

DAVIES. I got my papers there!

Pause.

ASTON. Your what?

DAVIES. I got my papers there!

Pause.

ASTON. What are they doing at Sidcup?

DAVIES. A man I know has got them. I left them with him. You see? They prove who I am! I can't move without them papers. They tell you who I am. You see! I'm stuck without them.

ASTON. Why's that?

DAVIES. You see, what it is, you see, I changed my name!

Years ago. I been going around under an assumed name!
That's not my real name.

ASTON. What name you been going under?

DAVIES. Jenkins. Bernard Jenkins. That's my name. That's
the name I'm known, anyway. But it's no good me going on
with that name. I got no rights. I got an insurance card here.
(*He takes a card from his pocket.*) Under the name of Jenkins.
See? Bernard Jenkins. Look. It's got four stamps on it. Four
of them. But I can't go along with these. That's not my real
name, they'd find out, they'd have me in the nick. Four
stamps. I haven't paid out pennies, I've paid out pounds.
I've paid out pounds, not pennies. There's been other
stamps, plenty, but they haven't put them on, the nigs, I
never had enough time to go into it.

ASTON. They should have stamped your card.

DAVIES. It would have done no good! I'd have got nothing
anyway. That's not my real name. If I take that card along I
go in the nick.

ASTON. What's your real name, then?

DAVIES. Davies. Mac Davies. That was before I changed my
name.

   Pause.

ASTON. It looks as though you want to sort all that out.

DAVIES. If only I could get down to Sidcup! I've been waiting
for the weather to break. He's got my papers, this man I left
them with, it's got it all down there, I could prove everything.

ASTON. How long's he had them?

DAVIES. What?

ASTON. How long's he had them?

DAVIES. Oh, must be . . . it was in the war . . . must be
. . . about near on fifteen year ago.

   He suddenly becomes aware of the bucket and looks up.

ASTON. Any time you want to . . . get into bed, just get in.
Don't worry about me.

DAVIES (*taking off his overcoat*). Eh, well, I think I will. I'm a bit . . . a bit done in. (*He steps out of his trousers, and holds them out.*) Shall I put these on here?

ASTON. Yes.

> DAVIES *puts the coat and trousers on the clothes horse.*

DAVIES. I see you got a bucket up here.

ASTON. Leak.

> DAVIES *looks up.*

DAVIES. Well, I'll try your bed then. You getting in?

ASTON. I'm mending this plug.

> DAVIES *looks at him and then at the gas stove.*

DAVIES. You . . . you can't move this, eh?

ASTON. Bit heavy.

DAVIES. Yes.

> DAVIES *gets into bed. He tests his weight and length.*

Not bad. Not bad. A fair bed. I think I'll sleep in this.

ASTON. I'll have to fix a proper shade on that bulb. The light's a bit glaring.

DAVIES. Don't you worry about that, mister, don't you worry about that. (*He turns and puts the cover up.*)

> ASTON *sits, poking his plug.*
> *The* LIGHTS FADE OUT. *Darkness.*
> LIGHTS UP. *Morning.*
> ASTON *is fastening his trousers, standing by the bed. He straightens his bed. He turns, goes to the centre of the room and looks at* DAVIES. *He turns, puts his jacket on, turns, goes towards* DAVIES *and looks down on him.*
> *He coughs.* DAVIES *sits up abruptly.*

DAVIES. What? What's this? What's this?

ASTON. It's all right.

DAVIES (*staring*). What's this?

ASTON. It's all right.

> DAVIES *looks about.*

DAVIES. Oh, yes.

> ASTON *goes to his bed, picks up the plug and shakes it.*

ASTON. Sleep well?

DAVIES. Yes. Dead out. Must have been dead out.

> ASTON *goes downstage right, collects the toaster and examines it.*

ASTON. You . . . er. . . .

DAVIES. Eh?

ASTON. Were you dreaming or something?

DAVIES. Dreaming?

ASTON. Yes.

DAVIES. I don't dream. I've never dreamed.

ASTON. No, nor have I.

DAVIES. Nor me.

> *Pause.*

Why you ask me that, then?

ASTON. You were making noises.

DAVIES. Who was?

ASTON. You were.

> DAVIES *gets out of bed. He wears long underpants.*

DAVIES. Now, wait a minute. Wait a minute, what do you mean? What kind of noises?

ASTON. You were making groans. You were jabbering.

DAVIES. Jabbering? Me?

ASTON. Yes.

DAVIES. I don't jabber, man. Nobody ever told me that before.

> *Pause.*

What would I be jabbering about?

ASTON. I don't know.

DAVIES. I mean, where's the sense in it?

> *Pause.*

Nobody ever told me that before.

> *Pause.*

You got hold of the wrong bloke, mate.

ASTON (*crossing to the bed with the toaster*). No. You woke me up. I thought you might have been dreaming.

DAVIES. I wasn't dreaming. I never had a dream in my life.

Pause.

ASTON. Maybe it was the bed.

DAVIES. Nothing wrong with this bed.

ASTON. Might be a bit unfamiliar.

DAVIES. There's nothing unfamiliar about me with beds. I slept in beds. I don't make noises just because I sleep in a bed. I slept in plenty of beds.

Pause.

I tell you what, maybe it were them Blacks.

ASTON. What?

DAVIES. Them noises.

ASTON. What Blacks?

DAVIES. Them you got. Next door. Maybe it were them Blacks making noises, coming up through the walls.

ASTON. Hmmnn.

DAVIES. That's my opinion.

ASTON *puts down the plug and moves to the door.*

Where you going, you going out?

ASTON. Yes.

DAVIES (*seizing the sandals*). Wait a minute then, just a minute.

ASTON. What you doing?

DAVIES (*putting on the sandals*). I better come with you.

ASTON. Why?

DAVIES. I mean, I better come out with you, anyway.

ASTON. Why?

DAVIES. Well . . . don't you want me to go out?

ASTON. What for?

DAVIES. I mean . . . when you're out. Don't you want me to get out . . . when you're out?

ASTON. You don't have to go out.

DAVIES. You mean . . . I can stay here?

ASTON. Do what you like. You don't have to come out just because I go out.

DAVIES. You don't mind me staying here?

ASTON. I've got a couple of keys. (*He goes to a box by his bed and finds them.*) This door and the front door. (*He hands them to* DAVIES.)

DAVIES. Thanks very much, the best of luck.

Pause. ASTON *stands.*

ASTON. I think I'll take a stroll down the road. A little . . . kind of a shop. Man there'd got a jig saw the other day. I quite liked the look of it.

DAVIES. A jig saw, mate?

ASTON. Yes. Could be very useful.

DAVIES. Yes.

Slight pause.

What's that then, exactly, then?

ASTON *walks up to the window and looks out.*

ASTON. A jig saw? Well, it comes from the same family as the fret saw. But it's an appliance, you see. You have to fix it on to a portable drill.

DAVIES. Ah, that's right. They're very handy.

ASTON. They are, yes.

Pause.

You know, I was sitting in a café the other day. I happened to be sitting at the same table as this woman. Well, we started to . . . we started to pick up a bit of a conversation. I don't know . . . about her holiday, it was, where she'd been. She'd been down to the south coast. I can't remember where though. Anyway, we were just sitting there, having this bit of a conversation . . . then suddenly she put her hand over to mine . . . and she said, how would you like me to have a look at your body?

DAVIES. Get out of it.

Pause.

ASTON. Yes. To come out with it just like that, in the middle of this conversation. Struck me as a bit odd.

DAVIES. They've said the same thing to me.

ASTON. Have they?

DAVIES. Women? There's many a time they've come up to me and asked me more or less the same question.

Pause.

ASTON. What did you say your name was?

DAVIES. Bernard Jenkins is my assumed one.

ASTON. No, your other one?

DAVIES. Davies. Mac Davies.

ASTON. Welsh, are you?

DAVIES. Eh?

ASTON. You Welsh?

Pause.

DAVIES. Well, I been around, you know . . . what I mean . . . I been about. . . .

ASTON. Where were you born then?

DAVIES (darkly). What do you mean?

ASTON. Where were you born?

DAVIES. I was . . . uh . . . oh, it's a bit hard, like, to set your mind back . . . see what I mean . . . going back . . . . a good way . . . lose a bit of track, like . . . you know. . . .

ASTON (going to below the fireplace). See this plug? Switch it on here, if you like. This little fire.

DAVIES. Right, mister.

ASTON. Just plug in here.

DAVIES. Right, mister.

ASTON goes towards the door.
(Anxiously). What do I do?

ASTON. Just switch it on, that's all. The fire'll come on.

DAVIES. I tell you what. I won't bother about it.

ASTON. No trouble.

DAVIES. No, I don't go in for them things much.

ASTON. Should work. (*Turning*.) Right.

DAVIES. Eh, I was going to ask you, mister, what about this stove? I mean, do you think it's going to be letting out any . . . what do you think?

ASTON. It's not connected.

DAVIES. You see, the trouble is, it's right on top of my bed, you see? What I got to watch is nudging . . . one of them gas taps with my elbow when I get up, you get my meaning?

He goes round to the other side of stove and examines it.

ASTON. There's nothing to worry about.

DAVIES. Now look here, don't you worry about it. All I'll do, I'll keep an eye on these taps every now and again, like, you see. See they're switched off. You leave it to me.

ASTON. I don't think. . . .

DAVIES (*coming round*). Eh, mister, just one thing . . . eh . . . . you couldn't slip me a couple of bob, for a cup of tea, just, you know?

ASTON. I gave you a few bob last night.

DAVIES. Eh, so you did. So you did. I forgot. Went clean out of my mind. That's right. Thank you, mister. Listen. You're sure now, you're sure you don't mind me staying here? I mean, I'm not the sort of man who wants to take any liberties.

ASTON. No, that's all right.

DAVIES. I might get down to Wembley later on in the day.

ASTON. Uh-uh.

DAVIES. There's a caff down there, you see, might be able to get fixed up there. I was there, see? I know they were a bit short-handed. They might be in the need of a bit of staff.

ASTON. When was that?

DAVIES. Eh? Oh, well, that was . . . near on . . . that'll
be . . . that'll be a little while ago now. But of course what
it is, they can't find the right kind of people in these places.
What they want to do, they're trying to do away with these
foreigners, you see, in catering. They want an Englishman
to pour their tea, that's what they want, that's what they're
crying out for. It's only common sense, en't? Oh, I got all
that under way . . . that's . . . uh . . . that's . . . what
I'll be doing.

Pause.

If only I could get down there.

ASTON. Mmnn. (ASTON *moves to the door.*) Well, I'll be seeing
you then.

DAVIES. Yes. Right.

ASTON goes out and closes the door.

*DAVIES stands still. He waits a few seconds, then goes to the
door, opens it, looks out, closes it, stands with his back to it,
turns swiftly, opens it, looks out, comes back, closes the
door, finds the keys in his pocket, tries one, tries the other,
locks the door. He looks about the room. He then goes quickly
to ASTON'S bed, bends, brings out the pair of shoes and
examines them.*

Not a bad pair of shoes. Bit pointed.

*He puts them back under the bed. He examines the area by
ASTON'S bed, picks up a vase and looks into it, then picks
up a box and shakes it.*

Screws!

*He sees paint buckets at the top of the bed, goes to them, and
examines them.*

Paint. What's he going to paint?

*He puts the bucket down, comes to the centre of the room,
looks up at bucket, and grimaces.*

I'll have to find out about that. (*He crosses right, and picks up
a blow-lamp.*) He's got some stuff in here. (*He picks up the*

Buddha and looks at it.) Full of stuff. Look at all this. (*His eye falls on the piles of papers.*) What's he got all those papers for ? Damn pile of papers.

> *He goes to a pile and touches it. The pile wobbles. He steadies it.*

Hold it, hold it!

> *He holds the pile and pushes the papers back into place.*
> *The door opens.*
> MICK *comes in, puts the key in his pocket, and closes the door silently. He stands at the door and watches* DAVIES.

What's he got all these papers for ? (DAVIES *climbs over the rolled carpet to the blue case.*) Had a sheet and pillow ready in here. (*He opens the case.*) Nothing. (*He shuts the case.*) Still, I had a sleep though. I don't make no noises. (*He looks at the window.*) What's this ?

> *He picks up another case and tries to open it.* MICK *moves up-stage, silently.*

Locked. (*He puts it down and moves downstage.*) Must be something in it. (*He picks up a sideboard drawer, rummages in the contents, then puts it down.*)

> MICK *slides across the room.*
> DAVIES *half turns,* MICK *seizes his arm and forces it up his back.* DAVIES *screams.*

Uuuuuuuhhh! Uuuuuuuhhh! What! What! What! Uuuuuuuhhh!

> MICK *swiftly forces him to the floor, with* DAVIES *struggling, grimacing, whimpering and staring.*
> MICK *holds his arm, puts his other hand to his lips, then puts his hand to* DAVIES' *lips.* DAVIES *quietens.* MICK *lets him go.* DAVIES *writhes.* MICK *holds out a warning finger. He then squats down to regard* DAVIES. *He regards him, then stands looking down on him.* DAVIES *massages his arm, watching* MICK. MICK *turns slowly to look at the room. He goes to* DAVIES' *bed and uncovers it. He turns, goes to the*

clothes horse and picks up DAVIES' *trousers.* DAVIES *starts to rise.* MICK *presses him down with his foot and stands over him. Finally he removes his foot. He examines the trousers and throws them back.* DAVIES *remains on the floor, crouched.* MICK *slowly goes to the chair, sits, and watches* DAVIES, *expressionless.*
Silence.

MICK. What's the game?

Curtain.

Act Two

A few seconds later.

> MICK *is seated,* DAVIES *on the floor, half seated, crouched.*
> *Silence.*

MICK. Well?

DAVIES. Nothing, nothing. Nothing.

> *A drip sounds in the bucket overhead. They look up.* MICK
> *looks back to* DAVIES.

MICK. What's your name?

DAVIES. I don't know you. I don't know who you are.

> *Pause.*

MICK. Eh?

DAVIES. Jenkins.

MICK. Jenkins?

DAVIES. Yes.

MICK. Jen . . . kins.

> *Pause.*

> You sleep here last night?

DAVIES. Yes.

MICK. Sleep well?

DAVIES. Yes.

MICK. I'm awfully glad. It's awfully nice to meet you.

> *Pause.*

> What did you say your name was?

DAVIES. Jenkins.

MICK. I beg your pardon?

DAVIES. Jenkins!

> *Pause.*

MICK. Jen . . . kins.

A drip sounds in the bucket. DAVIES *looks up.*

You remind me of my uncle's brother. He was always on the move, that man. Never without his passport. Had an eye for the girls. Very much your build. Bit of an athlete. Long-jump specialist. He had a habit of demonstrating different run-ups in the drawing-room round about Christmas time. Had a penchant for nuts. That's what it was. Nothing else but a penchant. Couldn't eat enough of them. Peanuts, walnuts, brazil nuts, monkey nuts, wouldn't touch a piece of fruit cake. Had a marvellous stop-watch. Picked it up in Hong Kong. The day after they chucked him out of the Salvation Army. Used to go in number four for Beckenham Reserves. That was before he got his Gold Medal. Had a funny habit of carrying his fiddle on his back. Like a papoose. I think there was a bit of the Red Indian in him. To be honest, I've never made out how he came to be my uncle's brother. I've often thought that maybe it was the other way round. I mean that my uncle was his brother and he was my uncle. But I never called him uncle. As a matter of fact I called him Sid. My mother called him Sid too. It was a funny business. Your spitting image he was. Married a Chinaman and went to Jamaica.

Pause.

I hope you slept well last night.

DAVIES. Listen! I don't know who you are!

MICK. What bed you sleep in?

DAVIES. Now look here—

MICK. Eh?

DAVIES. That one.

MICK. Not the other one?

DAVIES. No.

MICK. Choosy.

Pause.

How do you like my room?

DAVIES. Your room?

MICK. Yes.

DAVIES. This ain't your room. I don't know who you are. I ain't never seen you before.

MICK. You know, believe it or not, you've got a funny kind of resemblance to a bloke I once knew in Shoreditch. Actually he lived in Aldgate. I was staying with a cousin in Camden Town. This chap, he used to have a pitch in Finsbury Park, just by the bus depot. When I got to know him I found out he was brought up in Putney. That didn't make any difference to me. I know quite a few people who were born in Putney. Even if they weren't born in Putney they were born in Fulham. The only trouble was, he wasn't born in Putney, he was only brought up in Putney. It turned out he was born in the Caledonian Road, just before you get to the Nag's Head. His old mum was still living at the Angel. All the buses passed right by the door. She could get a 38, 581, 30 or 38A, take her down the Essex Road to Dalston Junction in next to no time. Well, of course, if she got the 30 he'd take her up Upper Street way, round by Highbury Corner and down to St. Paul's Church, but she'd get to Dalston Junction just the same in the end. I used to leave my bike in her garden on my way to work. Yes, it was a curious affair. Dead spit of you he was. Bit bigger round the nose but there was nothing in it.

> *Pause.*

Did you sleep here last night?

DAVIES. Yes.

MICK. Sleep well?

DAVIES. Yes!

MICK. Did you have to get up in the night?

DAVIES. No!

> *Pause.*

MICK. What's your name?

DAVIES (*shifting, about to rise*). Now look here!

MICK. What?

DAVIES. Jenkins!

MICK. Jen . . . kins.

> DAVIES *makes a sudden move to rise. A violent bellow from* MICK *sends him back.*

(*A shout.*) Sleep here last night?

DAVIES. Yes. . . .

MICK (*continuing at a great pace*). How'd you sleep?

DAVIES. I slept—

MICK. Sleep well?

DAVIES. Now look—

MICK. What bed?

DAVIES. That—

MICK. Not the other?

DAVIES. No!

MICK. Choosy.

> *Pause.*

(*Quietly.*) Choosy.

> *Pause.*

(*Again amiable.*) What sort of sleep did you have in that bed?

DAVIES (*banging the floor*). All right!

MICK. You weren't uncomfortable?

DAVIES (*groaning*). All right!

> MICK *stands, and moves to him.*

MICK. You a foreigner?

DAVIES. No.

MICK. Born and bred in the British Isles?

DAVIES. I was!

MICK. What did they teach you?

> *Pause.*

How did you like my bed?

> *Pause.*

That's my bed. You want to mind you don't catch a draught.

DAVIES. From the bed?

MICK. No, now, up your arse.

> DAVIES *stares warily at* MICK, *who turns.* DAVIES
> *scrambles to the clothes horse and seizes his trousers.* MICK
> *turns swiftly and grabs them.* DAVIES *lunges for them.*
> MICK *holds out a hand, warningly.*

You intending to settle down here?

DAVIES. Give me my trousers then.

MICK. You settling down for a long stay?

DAVIES. Give me my bloody trousers!

MICK. Why, where you going?

DAVIES. Give me and I'm going, I'm going to Sidcup!

> MICK *flicks the trousers in* DAVIES' *face several times.*
> DAVIES *retreats.*
>
> *Pause.*

MICK. You know, you remind me of a bloke I bumped into once, just the other side of the Guildford by-pass—

DAVIES. I was brought here!

> *Pause.*

MICK. Pardon?

DAVIES. I was brought here! I was brought here!

MICK. Brought here? Who brought you here?

DAVIES. Man who lives here . . . he. . . .

> *Pause.*

MICK. Fibber.

DAVIES. I was brought here, last night . . . met him in a caff . . . I was working . . . I got the bullet . . . I was working there . . . bloke saved me from a punch up, brought me here, brought me right here.

> *Pause.*

MICK. I'm afraid you're a born fibber, en't you? You're speaking to the owner. This is my room. You're standing in my house.

DAVIES. It's his . . . he seen me all right . . . he. . . .

MICK (*pointing to* DAVIES' *bed*). That's my bed.

DAVIES. What about that, then?

MICK. That's my mother's bed.

DAVIES. Well she wasn't in it last night!

MICK (*moving to him*). Now don't get perky, son, don't get perky. Keep your hands off my old mum.

DAVIES. I ain't . . . I haven't. . . .

MICK. Don't get out of your depth, friend, don't start taking liberties with my old mother, let's have a bit of respect.

DAVIES. I got respect, you won't find anyone with more respect.

MICK. Well, stop telling me all these fibs.

DAVIES. Now listen to me, I never seen you before, have I?

MICK. Never seen my mother before either, I suppose?

> *Pause.*

I think I'm coming to the conclusion that you're an old rogue. You're nothing but an old scoundrel.

DAVIES. Now wait—

MICK. Listen, son. Listen, sonny. You stink.

DAVIES. You ain't got no right to—

MICK. You're stinking the place out. You're an old robber, there's no getting away from it. You're an old skate. You don't belong in a nice place like this. You're an old barbarian. Honest. You got no business wandering about in an unfurnished flat. I could charge seven quid a week for this if I wanted to. Get a taker tomorrow. Three hundred and fifty a year exclusive. No argument. I mean, if that sort of money's in your range don't be afraid to say so. Here you are. Furniture and fittings, I'll take four hundred or the nearest offer. Rateable value ninety quid for the annum. You can reckon water, heating and lighting at close on fifty. That'll cost you eight hundred and ninety if you're all that keen. Say the word and I'll have my solicitors draft you out a contract. Otherwise I've got the van outside, I can run you

to the police station in five minutes, have you in for tres-
passing, loitering with intent, daylight robbery, filching,
thieving and stinking the place out. What do you say?
Unless you're really keen on a straightforward purchase. Of
course, I'll get my brother to decorate it up for you first. I've
got a brother who's a number one decorator. He'll decorate
it up for you. If you want more space, there's four more
rooms along the landing ready to go. Bathroom, living-
room, bedroom and nursery. You can have this as your
study. This brother I mentioned, he's just about to start on
the other rooms. Yes, just about to start. So what do you
say? Eight hundred odd for this room or three thousand
down for the whole upper storey. On the other hand, if you
prefer to approach it in the long-term way I know an
insurance firm in West Ham'll be pleased to handle the
deal for you. No strings attached, open and above board,
untarnished record; twenty per cent interest, fifty per cent
deposit; down payments, back payments, family allowances,
bonus schemes, remission of term for good behaviour, six
months lease, yearly examination of the relevant archives,
tea laid on, disposal of shares, benefit extension, compen-
sation on cessation, comprehensive indemnity against Riot,
Civil Commotion, Labour Disturbances, Storm, Tempest,
Thunderbolt, Larceny or Cattle all subject to a daily check
and double check. Of course we'd need a signed declaration
from your personal medical attendant as assurance that you
possess the requisite fitness to carry the can, won't we?
Who do you bank with?

Pause.

Who do you bank with?

The door opens. ASTON *comes in.* MICK *turns and drops the
trousers.* DAVIES *picks them up and puts them on.* ASTON,
*after a glance at the other two, goes to his bed, places a bag
which he is carrying on it, sits down and resumes fixing the
toaster.* DAVIES *retreats to his corner.* MICK *sits in the chair*

Silence.
A drip sounds in the bucket. They all look up.
Silence.

You still got that leak.

ASTON. Yes.

Pause.

It's coming from the roof.

MICK. From the roof, eh?

ASTON. Yes.

Pause.

I'll have to tar it over.

MICK. You're going to tar it over?

ASTON. Yes.

MICK. What?

ASTON. The cracks.

Pause.

MICK. You'll be tarring over the cracks on the roof.

ASTON. Yes.

Pause.

MICK. Think that'll do it?

ASTON. It'll do it, for the time being.

MICK. Uh.

Pause.

DAVIES (*abruptly*). What do you do—?

They both look at him.

What do you do . . . when that bucket's full?

Pause.

ASTON. Empty it.

Pause.

MICK. I was telling my friend you were about to start decorating the other rooms.

ASTON. Yes.
> *Pause.*
(*To* DAVIES.) I got your bag.

DAVIES. Oh. (*Crossing to him and taking it.*) Oh thanks, mister, thanks. Give it to you, did they?

> DAVIES *crosses back with the bag.*
> MICK *rises and snatches it.*

MICK. What's this?

DAVIES. Give us it, that's my bag!

MICK (*warding him off*). I've seen this bag before.

DAVIES. That's my bag!

MICK (*eluding him*). This bag's very familiar.

DAVIES. What do you mean?

MICK. Where'd you get it?

ASTON (*rising, to them*). Scrub it.

DAVIES. That's mine.

MICK. Whose?

DAVIES. It's mine! Tell him it's mine!

MICK. This your bag?

DAVIES. Give me it!

ASTON. Give it to him.

MICK. What? Give him what?

DAVIES. That bloody bag!

MICK (*slipping it behind the gas stove*). What bag? (*To* DAVIES.) What bag?

DAVIES (*moving*). Look here!

MICK (*facing him*). Where you going?

DAVIES. I'm going to get . . . my old . . .

MICK. Watch your step, sonny! You're knocking at the door when no one's at home. Don't push it too hard. You come busting into a private house, laying your hands on anything you can lay your hands on. Don't overstep the mark, son.

> ASTON *picks up the bag.*

DAVIES. You thieving bastard . . . you thieving skate . . .
let me get my——

ASTON. Here you are. (ASTON *offers the bag to* DAVIES.)

> MICK *grabs it.* ASTON *takes it.*
> MICK *grabs it.* DAVIES *reaches for it.*
> ASTON *takes it.* MICK *reaches for it.*
> ASTON *gives it to* DAVIES. MICK *grabs it.*
> *Pause.*
> ASTON *takes it.* DAVIES *takes it.* MICK *takes it.* DAVIES
> *reaches for it.* ASTON *takes it.*
> *Pause.*
> ASTON *gives it to* MICK. MICK *gives it to* DAVIES.
> DAVIES *grasps it to him.*
> *Pause.*
> MICK *looks at* ASTON. DAVIES *moves away with the bag.*
> *He drops it.*
> *Pause.*
> *They watch him. He picks it up. Goes to his bed, and sits.*
> ASTON *goes to his bed, sits, and begins to roll a cigarette.*
> MICK *stands still.*
> *Pause.*
> *A drip sounds in the bucket. They all look up.*
> *Pause.*

How did you get on at Wembley?

DAVIES. Well, I didn't get down there.

> *Pause.*

No. I couldn't make it.

> MICK *goes to the door and exits.*

ASTON. I had a bit of bad luck with that jig saw. When I got
there it had gone.

> *Pause.*

DAVIES. Who was that feller?

ASTON. He's my brother.

DAVIES. Is he? He's a bit of a joker, en' he?

ASTON. Uh.

DAVIES. Yes . . . he's a real joker.

ASTON. He's got a sense of humour.

DAVIES. Yes, I noticed.

> *Pause.*

He's a real joker, that lad, you can see that.

> *Pause.*

ASTON. Yes, he tends . . . he tends to see the funny side of things.

DAVIES. Well, he's got a sense of humour, en' he?

ASTON. Yes.

DAVIES. Yes, you could tell that.

> *Pause.*

I could tell the first time I saw him he had his own way of looking at things.

> ASTON *stands, goes to the sideboard drawer, right, picks up the statue of Buddha, and puts it on the gas stove.*

ASTON. I'm supposed to be doing up the upper part of the house for him.

DAVIES. What . . . you mean . . . you mean it's his house?

ASTON. Yes. I'm supposed to be decorating this landing for him. Make a flat out of it.

DAVIES. What does he do, then?

ASTON. He's in the building trade. He's got his own van.

DAVIES. He don't live here, do he?

ASTON. Once I get that shed up outside . . . I'll be able to give a bit more thought to the flat, you see. Perhaps I can knock up one or two things for it. (*He walks to the window.*) I can work with my hands, you see. That's one thing I can do. I never knew I could. But I can do all sorts of things now, with my hands. You know, manual things. When I get that shed up out there . . . I'll have a workshop, you see. I . . . could do a bit of woodwork. Simple woodwork, to start. Working with . . . good wood.

Pause.

Of course, there's a lot to be done to this place. What I think, though, I think I'll put in a partition . . . in one of the rooms along the landing. I think it'll take it. You know . . . they've got these screens . . . you know . . . Oriental. They break up a room with them. Make it into two parts. I could either do that or I could have a partition. I could knock them up, you see, if I had a workshop.

Pause.

Anyway, I think I've decided on the partition.

Pause.

DAVIES. Eh, look here, I been thinking. This ain't my bag.

ASTON. Oh. No.

DAVIES. No, this ain't my bag. My bag, it was another kind of bag altogether, you see. I know what they've done. What they done, they kept my bag, and they given you another one altogether.

ASTON. No . . . what happened was, someone had gone off with your bag.

DAVIES (*rising*). That's what I said!

ASTON. Anyway, I picked that bag up somewhere else. It's got a few . . . pieces of clothes in it too. He let me have the whole lot cheap.

DAVIES (*opening the bag*). Any shoes?

    DAVIES *takes two check shirts, bright red and bright green, from the bag. He holds them up.*

Check.

ASTON. Yes.

DAVIES. Yes . . . well, I know about these sort of shirts, you see. Shirts like these, they don't go far in the wintertime. I mean, that's one thing I know for a fact. No, what I need, is a kind of a shirt with stripes, a good solid shirt, with stripes going down. That's what I want. (*He takes from the bag a deep-red velvet smoking-jacket.*) What's this?

ASTON. It's a smoking-jacket.

DAVIES. A smoking-jacket? (*He feels it.*) This ain't a bad piece of cloth. I'll see how it fits.

He tries it on.

You ain't got a mirror here, have you?

ASTON. I don't think I have.

DAVIES. Well, it don't fit too bad. How do you think it looks?

ASTON. Looks all right.

DAVIES. Well, I won't say no to this, then.

ASTON *picks up the plug and examines it.*

No, I wouldn't say no to this.

Pause.

ASTON. You could be . . . caretaker here, if you liked.

DAVIES. What?

ASTON. You could . . . look after the place, if you liked . . . you know, the stairs and the landing, the front steps, keep an eye on it. Polish the bells.

DAVIES. Bells?

ASTON. I'll be fixing a few, down by the front door. Brass.

DAVIES. Caretaking, eh?

ASTON. Yes.

DAVIES. Well, I . . . I never done caretaking before, you know . . . I mean to say . . . I never . . . what I mean to say is . . . I never been a caretaker before.

Pause.

ASTON. How do you feel about being one, then?

DAVIES. Well, I reckon . . . Well, I'd have to know . . . you know. . . .

ASTON. What sort of. . . .

DAVIES. Yes, what sort of . . . you know. . . .

Pause.

ASTON. Well, I mean. . . .

DAVIES. I mean, I'd have to . . . I'd have to. . . .

ASTON. Well, I could tell you. . . .

DAVIES. That's . . . that's it . . . you see . . . you get my meaning?

ASTON. When the time comes. . . .

DAVIES. I mean, that's what I'm getting at, you see. . . .

ASTON. More or less exactly what you. . . .

DAVIES. You see, what I mean to say . . . what I'm getting at is . . . I mean, what sort of jobs. . . .

Pause.

ASTON. Well, there's things like the stairs . . . and the . . . the bells. . . .

DAVIES. But it'd be a matter . . . wouldn't it . . . it'd be a matter of a broom . . . isn't it?

ASTON. Yes, and of course, you'd need a few brushes.

DAVIES. You'd need implements . . . you see . . . you'd need a good few implements. . . .

ASTON *takes a white overall from a nail over his bed, and shows it to* DAVIES.

ASTON. You could wear this, if you liked.

DAVIES. Well . . . that's nice, en't?

ASTON. It'd keep the dust off.

DAVIES (*putting it on*). Yes, this'd keep the dust off, all right. Well off. Thanks very much, mister.

ASTON. You see, what we could do, we could . . . I could fit a bell at the bottom, outside the front door, with "Caretaker" on it. And you could answer any queries.

DAVIES. Oh, I don't know about that.

ASTON. Why not?

DAVIES. Well, I mean, you don't know who might come up them front steps, do you? I got to be a bit careful.

ASTON. Why, someone after you?

DAVIES. After me? Well, I could have that Scotch git coming looking after me, couldn't I? All I'd do, I'd hear the bell, I'd go down there, open the door, who might be there, any Harry

might be there. I could be buggered as easy as that, man.
They might be there after my card, I mean look at it, here
I am, I only got four stamps, on this card, here it is, look,
four stamps, that's all I got, I ain't got any more, that's all I
got, they ring the bell called Caretaker, they'd have me in,
that's what they'd do, I wouldn't stand a chance. Of course
I got plenty of other cards lying about, but they don't know
that, and I can't tell them, can I, because then they'd find
out I was going about under an assumed name. You see, the
name I call myself now, that's not my real name. My real
name's not the one I'm using, you see. It's different. You
see, the name I go under now ain't my real one. It's assumed.

Silence.
THE LIGHTS FADE TO BLACKOUT.
THEN UP TO DIM LIGHT THROUGH THE WINDOW.
A door bangs.
Sound of a key in the door of the room.
DAVIES *enters, closes the door, and tries the light switch,*
on, off, on, off.

DAVIES (*muttering*). What's this? (*He switches on and off.*)
What's the matter with this damn light? (*He switches on and*
off.) Aaah. Don't tell me the damn light's gone now.
   Pause.
What'll I do? Damn light's gone now. Can't see a thing.
   Pause.
What'll I do now? (*He moves, stumbles.*) Ah God, what's
that? Give me a light. Wait a minute.
   He feels for matches in his pocket, takes out a box and lights
   one. The match goes out. The box falls.
Aah! Where is it? (*Stooping.*) Where's the bloody box?
   The box is kicked.
What's that? What? Who's that? What's that?
   Pause. He moves.

Where's my box? It was down here. Who's this? Who's
moving it?

Silence.

Come on. Who's this? Who's this got my box?

Pause.

Who's in here!

Pause.

I got a knife here. I'm ready. Come on then, who are you?

He moves, stumbles, falls and cries out.

Silence.

A faint whimper from DAVIES. *He gets up.*

All right!

He stands. Heavy breathing.

*Suddenly the electrolux starts to hum. A figure moves with it,
guiding it. The nozzle moves along the floor after* DAVIES,
who skips, dives away from it and falls, breathlessly.

Ah, ah, ah, ah, ah, ah! Get away-y-y-y-y!

The electrolux stops. The figure jumps on ASTON'S *bed.*

I'm ready for you! I'm . . . I'm . . . I'm here!

*The figure takes out the electrolux plug from the light socket
and fits the bulb. The light goes on.* DAVIES *flattens himself
against right wall, knife in hand.* MICK *stands on the bed,
holding the plug.*

MICK. I was just doing some spring cleaning. (*He gets down.*)
There used to be a wall plug for this electrolux. But it
doesn't work. I had to fit it in the light socket. (*He puts the
electrolux under* ASTON'S *bed.*) How do you think the place
is looking? I gave it a good going over.

Pause.

We take it in turns, once a fortnight, my brother and me, to
give the place a thorough going over. I was working late tonight, I only just got here. But I thought I better get on with
it, as it's my turn.

Pause.

It's not that I actually live here. I don't. As a matter of fact I live somewhere else. But after all, I'm responsible for the upkeep of the premises, en' I? Can't help being house-proud.

He moves towards DAVIES *and indicates the knife.*

What are you waving that about for?

DAVIES. You come near me. . . .

MICK. I'm sorry if I gave you a start. But I had you in mind too, you know. I mean, my brother's guest. We got to think of your comfort, en't we? Don't want the dust to get up your nose. How long you thinking of staying here, by the way? As a matter of fact, I was going to suggest that we'd lower your rent, make it just a nominal sum, I mean until you get fixed up. Just nominal, that's all.

Pause.

Still, if you're going to be spiky, I'll have to reconsider the whole proposition.

Pause.

Eh, you're not thinking of doing any violence on me, are you? You're not the violent sort, are you?

DAVIES (*vehemently*). I keep myself to myself, mate. But if anyone starts with me though, they know what they got coming.

MICK. I can believe that.

DAVIES. You do. I been all over, see? You understand my meaning? I don't mind a bit of a joke now and then, but anyone'll tell you . . . that no one starts anything with me.

MICK. I get what you mean, yes.

DAVIES. I can be pushed so far . . . but. . . .

MICK. No further.

DAVIES. That's it.

MICK *sits on junk down right.*

What you doing?

MICK. No, I just want to say that . . . I'm very impressed by that.

DAVIES. Eh?

MICK. I'm very impressed by what you've just said.

Pause.

Yes, that's impressive, that is.

Pause.

I'm impressed, anyway.

DAVIES. You know what I'm talking about, then?

MICK. Yes, I know. I think we understand one another.

DAVIES. Uh? Well . . . I'll tell you . . . I'd . . . I'd like to think that. You been playing me about, you know. I don't know why. I never done you no harm.

MICK. No, you know what it was? We just got off on the wrong foot. That's all it was.

DAVIES. Ay, we did.

DAVIES *joins* MICK *in junk.*

MICK. Like a sandwich?

DAVIES. What?

MICK (*taking a sandwich from his pocket.*) Have one of these.

DAVIES. Don't you pull anything.

MICK. No, you're still not understanding me. I can't help being interested in any friend of my brother's. I mean, you're my brother's friend, aren't you?

DAVIES. Well, I . . . I wouldn't put it as far as that.

MICK. Don't you find him friendly, then?

DAVIES. Well, I wouldn't say we was all that friends. I mean, he done me no harm, but I wouldn't say he was any particular friend of mine. What's in that sandwich, then?

MICK. Cheese.

DAVIES. That'll do me.

MICK. Take one.

DAVIES. Thank you, mister.

MICK. I'm sorry to hear my brother's not very friendly.

DAVIES. He's friendly, he's friendly, I didn't say he wasn't. . . .

MICK (*taking a salt-cellar from his pocket*). Salt?

DAVIES. No thanks. (*He munches the sandwich.*) I just can't exactly . . . make him out.

MICK (*feeling in his pocket*). I forgot the pepper.

DAVIES. Just can't get the hang of him, that's all.

MICK. I had a bit of beetroot somewhere. Must have mislaid it.

> *Pause.*

> DAVIES *chews the sandwich.* MICK *watches him eat. He then rises and strolls downstage.*

Uuh . . . listen . . . can I ask your advice? I mean, you're a man of the world. Can I ask your advice about something?

DAVIES. You go right ahead.

MICK. Well, what is it, you see, I'm . . . I'm a bit worried about my brother.

DAVIES. Your brother?

MICK. Yes . . . you see, his trouble is. . . .

DAVIES. What?

MICK. Well, it's not a very nice thing to say. . . .

DAVIES (*rising, coming downstage*). Go on now, you say it.

> MICK *looks at him.*

MICK. He doesn't like work.

> *Pause.*

DAVIES. Go on!

MICK. No, he just doesn't like work, that's his trouble.

DAVIES. Is that a fact?

MICK. It's a terrible thing to have to say about your own brother.

DAVIES. Ay.

MICK. He's just shy of it. Very shy of it.

DAVIES. I know that sort.

MICK. You know the type?

DAVIES. I've met them.

MICK. I mean, I want to get him going in the world.

DAVIES. Stands to reason, man.

MICK. If you got an older brother you want to push him on, you want to see him make his way. Can't have him idle, he's only doing himself harm. That's what I say.

DAVIES. Yes.

MICK. But he won't buckle down to the job.

DAVIES. He don't like work.

MICK. Work shy.

DAVIES. Sounds like it to me.

MICK. You've met the type, have you?

DAVIES. Me? I know that sort.

MICK. Yes.

DAVIES. I know that sort. I've met them.

MICK. Causing me great anxiety. You see, I'm a working man: I'm a tradesman. I've got my own van.

DAVIES. Is that a fact?

MICK. He's supposed to be doing a little job for me . . . I keep him here to do a little job . . . but I don't know . . . I'm coming to the conclusion he's a slow worker.

>   *Pause.*

What would your advice be?

DAVIES. Well . . . he's a funny bloke, your brother.

MICK. What?

DAVIES. I was saying, he's . . . he's a bit of a funny bloke; your brother.

>   MICK *stares at him.*

MICK. Funny? Why?

DAVIES. Well . . . he's funny. . . .

MICK. What's funny about him?

>   *Pause.*

DAVIES. Not liking work.

MICK. What's funny about that?

DAVIES. Nothing.

Pause.

MICK. I don't call it funny.

DAVIES. Nor me.

MICK. You don't want to start getting hypercritical.

DAVIES. No, no, I wasn't that, I wasn't . . . I was only saying. . . .

MICK. Don't get too glib.

DAVIES. Look, all I meant was—

MICK. Cut it! (*Briskly.*) Look! I got a proposition to make to you. I'm thinking of taking over the running of this place, you see? I think it could be run a bit more efficiently. I got a lot of ideas, a lot of plans. (*He eyes* DAVIES.) How would you like to stay on here, as caretaker?

DAVIES. What?

MICK. I'll be quite open with you. I could rely on a man like you around the place, keeping an eye on things.

DAVIES. Well now . . . wait a minute . . . I . . . I ain't never done no caretaking before, you know. . . .

MICK. Doesn't matter about that. It's just that you look a capable sort of man to me.

DAVIES. I am a capable sort of man. I mean to say, I've had plenty offers in my time, you know, there's no getting away from that.

MICK. Well, I could see before, when you took out that knife, that you wouldn't let anyone mess you about.

DAVIES. No one messes me about, man.

MICK. I mean, you've been in the services, haven't you?

DAVIES. The what?

MICK. You been in the services. You can tell by your stance.

DAVIES. Oh . . . yes. Spent half my life there, man. Overseas . . . like . . . serving . . . I was.

MICK. In the colonies, weren't you?

DAVIES. I was over there. I was one of the first over there.

MICK. That's it. You're just the man I been looking for.

DAVIES. What for?

MICK. Caretaker.

DAVIES. Yes, well . . . look . . . listen . . . who's the landlord here, him or you?

MICK. Me. I am. I got deeds to prove it.

DAVIES. Ah . . . (*Decisively.*) Well listen, I don't mind doing a bit of caretaking, I wouldn't mind looking after the place for you.

MICK. Of course, we'd come to a small financial agreement, mutually beneficial.

DAVIES. I leave you to reckon that out, like.

MICK. Thanks. There's only one thing.

DAVIES. What's that?

MICK. Can you give me any references?

DAVIES. Eh?

MICK. Just to satisfy my solicitor.

DAVIES. I got plenty of references. All I got to do is to go down to Sidcup tomorrow. I got all the references I want down there.

MICK. Where's that?

DAVIES. Sidcup. He ain't only got my references down there, he got all my papers down there. I know that place like the back of my hand. I'm going down there anyway, see what I mean, I got to get down there, or I'm done.

MICK. So we can always get hold of these references if we want them.

DAVIES. I'll be down there any day, I tell you. I was going down today, but I'm . . . I'm waiting for the weather to break.

MICK. Ah.

DAVIES. Listen. You can't pick me up a pair of good shoes, can you? I got a bad need for a good pair of shoes. I can't get anywhere without a pair of good shoes, see? Do you think there's any chance of you being able to pick me up a pair?

THE LIGHTS FADE TO BLACKOUT.

LIGHTS UP. *Morning.*

ASTON *is pulling on his trousers over long underwear. A slight grimace. He looks around at the head of his bed, takes a towel from the rail and waves it about. He pulls it down, goes to* DAVIES *and wakes him.* DAVIES *sits up abruptly.*

ASTON. You said you wanted me to get you up.

DAVIES. What for?

ASTON. You said you were thinking of going to Sidcup.

DAVIES. Ay, that'd be a good thing, if I got there.

ASTON. Doesn't look much of a day.

DAVIES. Ay, well, that's shot it, en't it?

ASTON. I . . . I didn't have a very good night again.

DAVIES. I slept terrible.

> *Pause.*

ASTON. You were making. . . .

DAVIES. Terrible. Had a bit of rain in the night, didn't it?

ASTON. Just a bit.

> *He goes to his bed, picks up a small plank and begins to sand-paper it.*

DAVIES. Thought so. Come in on my head.

> *Pause.*

Draught's blowing right in on my head, anyway.

> *Pause.*

Can't you close that window behind that sack?

ASTON. You could.

DAVIES. Well then, what about it, then? The rain's coming right in on my head.

ASTON. Got to have a bit of air.

> DAVIES *gets out of bed. He is wearing his trousers, waistcoat and vest.*

DAVIES (*putting on his sandals*). Listen. I've lived all my life in the air, boy. You don't have to tell me about air. What I'm saying is, there's too much air coming in that window when I'm asleep.

ASTON. Gets very stuffy in here without that window open.

ASTON *crosses to the chair, puts the plank on it, and continues sandpapering.*

DAVIES. Yes, but listen, you don't know what I'm telling you. That bloody rain, man, come right in on my head. Spoils my sleep. I could catch my death of cold with it, with that draught. That's all I'm saying. Just shut that window and no one's going to catch any colds, that's all I'm saying.

Pause.

ASTON. I couldn't sleep in here without that window open.

DAVIES. Yes, but what about me? What . . . what you got to say about my position?

ASTON. Why don't you sleep the other way round?

DAVIES. What do you mean?

ASTON. Sleep with your feet to the window.

DAVIES. What good would that do?

ASTON. The rain wouldn't come in on your head.

DAVIES. No, I couldn't do that. I couldn't do that.

Pause.

I mean, I got used to sleeping this way. It isn't me has to change, it's that window. You see, it's raining now. Look at it. It's coming down now.

Pause.

ASTON. I think I'll have a walk down to Goldhawk Road. I got talking to a man there. He had a saw bench. It looked in pretty good condition to me. Don't think it's much good to him.

Pause.

Have a walk down there, I think.

DAVIES. Listen to that. That's done my trip to Sidcup. Eh, what about closing that window now? It'll be coming in here.

ASTON. Close it for the time being.

DAVIES *closes the window and looks out.*

DAVIES. What's all that under that tarpaulin out there?

ASTON. Wood.

DAVIES. What for?

ASTON. To build my shed.

DAVIES *sits on his bed.*

DAVIES. You haven't come across that pair of shoes you was going to look out for me, have you?

ASTON. Oh. No. I'll see if I can pick some up today.

DAVIES. I can't go out in this with these, can I? I can't even go out and get a cup of tea.

ASTON. There's a café just along the road.

DAVIES. There may be, mate.

During ASTON'S *speech the room grows darker.*
By the close of the speech only ASTON *can be seen clearly.*
DAVIES *and all the objects are in the shadow. The fade-down of the light must be as gradual, as protracted and as unobtrusive as possible.*

ASTON. I used to go there quite a bit. Oh, years ago now. But I stopped. I used to like that place. Spent quite a bit of time in there. That was before I went away. Just before. I think that . . . place had a lot to do with it. They were all . . . a good bit older than me. But they always used to listen. I thought . . . they understood what I said. I mean I used to talk to them. I talked too much. That was my mistake. The same in the factory. Standing there, or in the breaks, I used to . . . talk about things. And these men, they used to listen, whenever I . . . had anything to say. It was all right. The trouble was, I used to have kind of hallucinations.

They weren't hallucinations, they . . . I used to get the feeling I could see things . . . very clearly . . . everything . . . was so clear . . . everything used . . . everything used to get very quiet . . . everything got very quiet . . . all this . . . quiet . . . and . . . this clear sight . . . it was . . . but maybe I was wrong. Anyway, someone must have said something. I didn't know anything about it. And . . . some kind of lie must have got around. And this lie went round. I thought people started being funny. In that café. The factory. I couldn't understand it. Then one day they took me to a hospital, right outside London. They . . . got me there. I didn't want to go. Anyway . . . I tried to get out, quite a few times. But . . . it wasn't very easy. They asked me questions, in there. Got me in and asked me all sorts of questions. Well, I told them . . . when they wanted to know . . . what my thoughts were. Hmmnn. Then one day . . . this man . . . doctor, I suppose . . . the head one . . . he was quite a man of . . . distinction . . . although I wasn't so sure about that. He called me in. He said . . . he told me I had something. He said they'd concluded their examination. That's what he said. And he showed me a pile of papers and he said that I'd got something, some complaint. He said . . . he just said that, you see. You've got . . . this thing. That's your complaint. And we've decided, he said, that in your interests there's only one course we can take. He said . . . but I can't . . . exactly remember . . . how he put it . . . he said, we're going to do something to your brain. He said . . . if we don't, you'll be in here for the rest of your life, but if we do, you stand a chance. You can go out, he said, and live like the others. What do you want to do to my brain, I said to him. But he just repeated what he'd said. Well, I wasn't a fool. I knew I was a minor. I knew he couldn't do anything to me without getting permission. I knew he had to get permission from my mother. So I wrote to her and told her

what they were trying to do. But she signed their form, you
see, giving them permission. I know that because he showed
me her signature when I brought it up. Well, that night I
tried to escape, that night. I spent five hours sawing at one
of the bars on the window in this ward. Right throughout
the dark. They used to shine a torch over the beds every
half hour. So I timed it just right. And then it was nearly
done, and a man had a . . . he had a fit, right next to me.
And they caught me, anyway. About a week later they
started to come round and do this thing to the brain. We
were all supposed to have it done, in this ward. And they
came round and did it one at a time. One a night. I was one
of the last. And I could see quite clearly what they did to the
others. They used to come round with these . . . I don't
know what they were . . . they looked like big pincers, with
wires on, the wires were attached to a little machine. It was
electric. They used to hold the man down, and this chief
. . . the chief doctor, used to fit the pincers, something like
earphones, he used to fit them on either side of the man's
skull. There was a man holding the machine, you see, and
he'd . . . There was a man holding the machine, you see,
and he'd turn it on, and the chief would just press these
pincers on either side of the skull and keep them there.
Then he'd take them off. They'd cover the man up . . .
and they wouldn't touch him again until later on. Some used
to put up a fight, but most of them didn't. They just lay
there. Well, they were coming round to me, and the night
they came I got up and stood against the wall. They told me
to get on the bed, and I knew they had to get me on the bed
because if they did it while I was standing up they might
break my spine. So I stood up and then one or two of them
came for me, well, I was younger then, I was much stronger
than I am now, I was quite strong then, I laid one of them
out and I had another one round the throat, and then
suddenly this chief had these pincers on my skull and I knew

he wasn't supposed to do it while I was standing up, that's why I . . . . . anyway, he did it. So I did get out. I got out of the place. . . . but I couldn't walk very well. I don't think my spine was damaged. That was perfectly all right. The trouble was . . . my thoughts . . . had become very slow . . . I couldn't think at all . . . I couldn't . . . get . . . my thoughts . . . together . . . uuuhh . . . I could . . . never quite get it . . . together. The trouble was, I couldn't hear what people were saying. I couldn't look to the right or the left, I had to look straight in front of me, because if I turned my head round . . . I couldn't keep . . . upright. And I had these headaches. I used to sit in my room. That was when I lived with my mother. And my brother. He was younger than me. And I laid everything out, in order, in my room, all the things I knew were mine, but I didn't die. The thing is, I should have been dead. I should have died. Anyway, I feel much better now. But I don't talk to people now. I steer clear of places like that café. I never go into them now. I don't talk to anyone . . . like that. I've often thought of going back and trying to find the man who did that to me. But I want to do something first. I want to build that shed out in the garden.

Curtain.

Act Three

Two weeks later.

MICK is lying on the floor, down left, his head resting on the rolled carpet, looking up at the ceiling.

DAVIES is sitting in the chair, holding his pipe. He is wearing the smoking-jacket. It is afternoon.

Silence.

DAVIES. I got a feeling he's done something to them cracks.

Pause.

See, there's been plenty of rain in the last week, but it ain't been dripping into the bucket.

Pause.

He must have tarred it over up there.

Pause.

There was someone walking about on the roof the other night. It must have been him.

Pause.

But I got a feeling he's tarred it over on the roof up there. Ain't said a word to me about it. Don't say a word to me.

Pause.

He don't answer me when I talk to him.

He lights a match, holds it to his pipe, and blows it.

He don't give me no knife!

Pause.

He don't give me no knife to cut my bread.

Pause.

How can I cut a loaf of bread without no knife?

Pause.

It's an impossibility.

Pause.

MICK. You've got a knife.

DAVIES. What?

MICK. You've got a knife.

DAVIES. I got a knife, sure I got a knife, but how do you expect me to cut a good loaf of bread with that? That's not a bread-knife. It's nothing to do with cutting bread. I picked it up somewhere. I don't know where it's been, do I? No, what I want—

MICK. I know what you want.

Pause. DAVIES *rises and goes to the gas stove.*

DAVIES. What about this gas stove? He tells me it's not connected. How do I know it's not connected? Here I am, I'm sleeping right with it, I wake up in the middle of the night, I'm looking right into the oven, man! It's right next to my face, how do I know, I could be lying there in bed, it might blow up, it might do me harm!

Pause.

But he don't seem to take any notice of what I say to him. I told him the other day, see, I told him about them Blacks, about them Blacks coming up from next door, and using the lavatory. I told him, it was all dirty in there, all the banisters were dirty, they were black, all the lavatory was black. But what did he do? He's supposed to be in charge of it here, he had nothing to say, he hadn't got a word to say.

Pause.

Couple of week ago . . . he sat there, he give me a long chat . . . about a couple of week ago. A long chat he give me. Since then he ain't said hardly a word. He went on talking there . . . I don't know what he was . . . he wasn't looking at me, he wasn't talking to me, he don't care about me. He was talking to himself! That's all he worries about. I mean, you come up to me, you ask my advice, he wouldn't never do a thing like that. I mean, we don't have any conversation, you see? You can't live in the same room with someone who . . . who don't have any conversation with you.

Pause.

I just can't get the hang of him.

Pause.

You and me, we could get this place going.

MICK (*ruminatively*). Yes, you're quite right. Look what I could do with this place.

Pause.

I could turn this place into a penthouse. For instance . . . this room. This room you could have as the kitchen. Right size, nice window, sun comes in. I'd have . . . I'd have teal-blue, copper and parchment linoleum squares. I'd have those colours re-echoed in the walls. I'd offset the kitchen units with charcoal-grey worktops. Plenty of room for cupboards for the crockery. We'd have a small wall cupboard, a large wall cupboard, a corner wall cupboard with revolving shelves. You wouldn't be short of cupboards. You could put the dining-room across the landing, see? Yes. Venetian blinds on the window, cork floor, cork tiles. You could have an off-white pile linen rug, a table in . . . in afromosia teak veneer, sideboard with matt black drawers, curved chairs with cushioned seats, armchairs in oatmeal tweed, a beech frame settee with a woven sea-grass seat, white-topped heat-resistant coffee table, white tile surround. Yes. Then the bedroom. What's a bedroom? It's a retreat. It's a place to go for rest and peace. So you want quiet decoration. The lighting functional. Furniture . . . mahogany and rosewood. Deep azure-blue carpet, unglazed blue and white curtains, a bedspread with a pattern of small blue roses on a white ground, dressing-table with a lift-up top containing a plastic tray, table lamp of white raffia . . . (MICK *sits up*) it wouldn't be a flat it'd be a palace.

DAVIES. I'd say it would, man.

MICK. A palace.

DAVIES. Who would live there?

MICK. I would. My brother and me.

   Pause.

DAVIES. What about me?

MICK (*quietly*). All this junk here, it's no good to anyone. It's just a lot of old iron, that's all. Clobber. You couldn't make a home out of this. There's no way you could arrange it. It's junk. He could never sell it, either, he wouldn't get tuppence for it.

   Pause.

Junk.

   Pause.

But he doesn't seem to be interested in what I got in mind, that's the trouble. Why don't you have a chat with him, see if he's interested?

DAVIES. Me?

MICK. Yes. You're a friend of his.

DAVIES. He's no friend of mine.

MICK. You're living in the same room with him, en't you?

DAVIES. He's no friend of mine. You don't know where you are with him. I mean, with a bloke like you, you know where you are.

   MICK *looks at him.*

I mean, you got your own ways, I'm not saying you ain't got your own ways, anyone can see that. You may have some funny ways, but that's the same with all of us, but with him it's different, see? I mean at least with you, the thing with you is you're . . .

MICK. Straightforward.

DAVIES. That's it, you're straightforward.

MICK. Yes.

DAVIES. But with him, you don't know what he's up to half the time!

MICK. Uh.

DAVIES. He's got no feelings!

Pause.

See, what I need is a clock! I need a clock to tell the time! How can I tell the time without a clock? I can't do it! I said to him, I said, look here, what about getting in a clock, so's I can tell what time it is? I mean, if you can't tell what time you're at you don't know where you are, you understand my meaning? See, what I got to do now, if I'm walking about outside, I got to get my eye on a clock, and keep the time in my head for when I come in. But that's no good, I mean I'm not in here five minutes and I forgotten it. I forgotten what time it was!

DAVIES *walks up and down the room.*

Look at it this way. If I don't feel well I have a bit of a lay down, then, when I wake up, I don't know what time it is to go and have a cup of tea! You see, it's not so bad when I'm coming in. I can see the clock on the corner, the moment I'm stepping into the house I know what the time is, but when I'm *in*! It's when I'm *in* . . . that I haven't the foggiest idea what time it is!

Pause.

No, what I need is a clock in here, in this room, and then I stand a bit of a chance. But he don't give me one.

DAVIES *sits in the chair.*

He wakes me up! He wakes me up in the middle of the night! Tells me I'm making noises! I tell you I've half a mind to give him a mouthful one of these days.

MICK. He don't let you sleep?

DAVIES. He don't let me sleep! He wakes me up!

MICK. That's terrible.

DAVIES. I been plenty of other places. They always let

me sleep. It's the same the whole world over. Except here.

MICK. Sleep's essential. I've always said that.

DAVIES. You're right, it's essential. I get up in the morning,
I'm worn out! I got business to see to. I got to move myself,
I got to sort myself out, I got to get fixed up. But when I
wake up in the morning I ain't got no energy in me. And on
top of that I ain't got no clock.

MICK. Yes.

DAVIES (*standing, moving*). He goes out, I don't know where he
goes to, where's he go, he never tells me. We used to have a
bit of a chat, not any more. I never see him, he goes out, he
comes in late, next thing I know he's shoving me about in the
middle of the night.

    Pause.

Listen! I wake up in the morning . . . I wake up in the
morning and he's smiling at me! He's standing there,
looking at me, smiling! I can see him, you see, I can see him
through the blanket. He puts on his coat, he turns himself
round, he looks down at my bed, there's a smile on his face!
What the hell's he smiling at? What he don't know is that
I'm watching him through that blanket. He don't know that!
He don't know I can see him, he thinks I'm asleep, but I got
my eye on him all the time through that blanket, see? But he
don't know that! He just looks at me and he smiles, but he
don't know that I can see him doing it!

    Pause.

(*Bending, close to* MICK.) No, what you want to do, you want
to speak to him, see? I got . . . I got that worked out. You
want to tell him . . . that we got ideas for this place, we
could build it up, we could get it started. You see, I could
decorate it out for you, I could give you a hand in doing it
. . . between us.

    Pause.

Where do you live now, then?

MICK. Me? Oh, I've got a little place. Not bad. Everything

laid on. You must come up and have a drink some time. Listen to some Tchaikovsky.

DAVIES. No, you see, you're the bloke who wants to talk to him. I mean, you're his brother.

Pause.

MICK. Yes . . . maybe I will.

A door bangs.
MICK *rises, goes to the door and exits.*

DAVIES. Where you going? This is him!

Silence.
DAVIES *stands, then goes to the window and looks out.*
ASTON *enters. He is carrying a paper bag. He takes off his overcoat, opens the bag and takes out a pair of shoes.*

ASTON. Pair of shoes.
DAVIES (*turning*). What?
ASTON. I picked them up. Try them.
DAVIES. Shoes? What sort?
ASTON. They might do you.

DAVIES *comes down stage, takes off his sandals and tries the shoes on. He walks about, waggling his feet, bends, and presses the leather.*

DAVIES. No, they're not right.
ASTON. Aren't they?
DAVIES. No, they don't fit.
ASTON. Mmnn.

Pause.

DAVIES. Well, I'll tell you what, they might do . . . until I get another pair.

Pause.

Where's the laces?
ASTON. No laces.
DAVIES. I can't wear them without laces.

ASTON. I just got the shoes.

DAVIES. Well now, look that puts the lid on it, don't it? I mean, you couldn't keep these shoes on right without a pair of laces. The only way to keep a pair of shoes on, if you haven't got no laces, is to tighten the foot, see? Walk about with a tight foot, see? Well, that's no good for the foot. Puts a bad strain on the foot. If you can do the shoes up proper there's less chance of you getting a strain.

ASTON *goes round to the top of his bed.*

ASTON. I might have some somewhere.

DAVIES. You see what I'm getting at?

Pause.

ASTON. Here's some. (*He hands them to* DAVIES.)

DAVIES. These are brown.

ASTON. That's all I got.

DAVIES. These shoes are black.

ASTON *does not answer.*

Well, they can do, anyway, until I get another pair.

DAVIES *sits in the chair and begins to lace his shoes.*

Maybe they'll get me down to Sidcup tomorrow. If I get down there I'll be able to sort myself out.

Pause.

I've been offered a good job. Man has offered it to me, he's . . . he's got plenty of ideas. He's got a bit of a future. But they want my papers, you see, they want my references. I'd have to get down to Sidcup before I could get hold of them. That's where they are, see. Trouble is, getting there. That's my problem. The weather's dead against it.

ASTON *quietly exits, unnoticed.*

Don't know as these shoes'll be much good. It's a hard road, I been down there before. Coming the other way, like. Last time I left there, it was . . . last time . . . getting on a while back . . . the road was bad, the rain was coming down, lucky I didn't die there on the road, but I got here, I kept going, all along . . . yes . . . I kept going all along. But all the same, I can't go on like this, what I got to do, I got to get back there, find this man—

He turns and looks about the room.

Christ! That bastard, he ain't even listening to me!

BLACKOUT.

DIM LIGHT THROUGH THE WINDOW.

It is night. ASTON *and* DAVIES *are in bed,* DAVIES *groaning.* ASTON *sits up, gets out of bed, switches on the light, goes over to* DAVIES *and shakes him.*

ASTON. Hey, stop it, will you? I can't sleep.

DAVIES. What? What? What's going on?

ASTON. You're making noises.

DAVIES. I'm an old man, what do you expect me to do, stop breathing?

ASTON. You're making noises.

DAVIES. What do you expect me to do, stop breathing?

ASTON goes to his bed, and puts on his trousers.

ASTON. I'll get a bit of air.

DAVIES. What do you expect me to do? I tell you, mate, I'm not surprised they took you in. Waking an old man up in the middle of the night, you must be off your nut! Giving me bad dreams, who's responsible, then, for me having bad dreams? If you wouldn't keep mucking me about I wouldn't make no noises! How do you expect me to sleep peaceful when you keep poking me all the time? What do you want me to do, stop breathing?

He throws the cover off and gets out of bed, wearing his vest, waistcoat and trousers.

It's getting so freezing in here I have to keep my trousers on to go to bed. I never done that before in my life. But that's

what I got to do here. Just because you won't put in any
bleeding heating! I've had just about enough with you
mucking me about. I've seen better days than you have, man.
Nobody ever got me inside one of them places, anyway. I'm
a sane man! So don't you start mucking me about. I'll be all
right as long as you keep your place. Just you keep your
place, that's all. Because I can tell you, your brother's got his
eye on you. He knows all about you. I got a friend there,
don't you worry about that. I got a true pal there. Treating
me like dirt! Why'd you invite me in here in the first place if
you was going to treat me like this? You think you're better
than me you got another think coming. I know enough.
They had you inside one of them places before, they can have
you inside again. Your brother's got his eye on you! They
can put the pincers on your head again, man! They can
have them on again! Any time. All they got to do is get the
word. They'd carry you in there, boy. They'd come here and
pick you up and carry you in! They'd keep you fixed! They'd
put them pincers on your head, they'd have you fixed!
They'd take one look at all this junk I got to sleep with they'd
know you were a creamer. That was the greatest mistake they
made, you take my tip, letting you get out of that place.
Nobody knows what you're at, you go out you come in,
nobody knows what you're at! Well, nobody messes me
about for long. You think I'm going to do your dirty work?
Haaaaahhhhh! You better think again! You want me to do
all the dirty work all up and down them stairs, just so I can
sleep in this lousy filthy hole every night? Not me, boy. Not
for you boy. You don't know what you're doing half the
time. You're up the creek! You're half off! You can tell it by
looking at you. Who ever saw you slip me a few bob?
Treating me like a bloody animal! I never been inside a
nuthouse!

ASTON *makes a slight move towards him.* DAVIES *takes his
knife from his back pocket.*

Don't come nothing with me, mate. I got this here. I used
it. I used it. Don't come it with me.

A pause. They stare at each other.

Mind what you do now.

Pause.

Don't you try anything with me.

Pause.

ASTON. I . . . I think it's about time you found somewhere
else. I don't think we're hitting it off.

DAVIES. Find somewhere else?

ASTON. Yes.

DAVIES. Me? You talking to me? Not me, man! You!

ASTON. What?

DAVIES. You! You better find somewhere else!

ASTON. I live here. You don't.

DAVIES. Don't I? Well, I live here. I been offered a job here.

ASTON. Yes . . . well, I don't think you're really suitable.

DAVIES. Not suitable? Well, I can tell you, there's someone
here thinks I am suitable. And I'll tell you. I'm staying on
here as caretaker! Get it! Your brother, he's told me, see,
he's told me the job is mine. Mine! So that's where I am.
I'm going to be his caretaker.

ASTON. My brother?

DAVIES. He's staying, he's going to run this place, and I'm
staying with him.

ASTON. Look. If I give you . . . a few bob you can get down
to Sidcup.

DAVIES. You build your shed first! A few bob! When I can
earn a steady wage here! You build your stinking shed first!
That's what!

ASTON stares at him.

ASTON. That's not a stinking shed.

Silence.

ASTON moves to him.

It's clean. It's all good wood. I'll get it up. No trouble.

DAVIES. Don't come too near!

ASTON. You've no reason to call that shed stinking.

DAVIES *points the knife.*

You stink.

DAVIES. What!

ASTON. You've been stinking the place out.

DAVIES. Christ, you say that to me!

ASTON. For days. That's one reason I can't sleep.

DAVIES. You call me that! You call me stinking!

ASTON. You better go.

DAVIES. I'LL STINK YOU!

He thrusts his arm out, the arm trembling, the knife pointing at ASTON'S *stomach.* ASTON *does not move. Silence.* DAVIES' *arm moves no further. They stand.*

I'll stink you. . . .

Pause.

ASTON. Get your stuff.

DAVIES *draws the knife in to his chest, breathing heavily.* ASTON *goes to* DAVIES' *bed, collects his bag and puts a few of* DAVIES' *things into it.*

DAVIES. You ain't . . . you ain't got the right . . . Leave that alone, that's mine!

DAVIES *takes the bag and presses the contents down.*

All right . . . I been offered a job here . . . you wait . . . (*He puts on his smoking-jacket.*) . . you wait . . . your brother . . . he'll sort you out . . . you call me that . . . you call me that . . . no one's ever called me that . . . (*He puts on his overcoat.*) You'll be sorry you called me that . . . . you ain't heard the last of this . . . (*He picks up his bag and goes to the door.*) You'll be sorry you called me that. . . .

He opens the door, ASTON *watching him.*

Now I know who I can trust.

DAVIES *goes out.* ASTON *stands.*
BLACKOUT.
LIGHTS UP. *Early evening.*
Voices on the stairs.
MICK *and* DAVIES *enter.*

DAVIES. Stink! You hear that! Me! I told you what he said, didn't I? Stink! You hear that? That's what he said to me!
MICK. Tch, tch, tch.
DAVIES. That's what he said to me.
MICK. You don't stink.
DAVIES. No, sir!
MICK. If you stank I'd be the first one to tell you.
DAVIES. I told him, I told him he . . . I said to him, you ain't heard the last of this man! I said, don't you forget your brother. I told him you'd be coming along to sort him out. He don't know what he's started, doing that. Doing that to me. I said to him, I said to him, he'll be along, your brother'll be along, he's got sense, not like you—
MICK. What do you mean?
DAVIES. Eh?
MICK. You saying my brother hasn't got any sense?
DAVIES. What? What I'm saying is, you got ideas for this place, all this . . . all this decorating, see? I mean, he's got no right to order me about. I take orders from you, I do my caretaking for you, I mean, you look upon me . . . you don't treat me like a lump of dirt . . . we can both . . . we can both see him for what he is.

  Pause.

MICK. What did he say then, when you told him I'd offered you the job as caretaker?
DAVIES. He . . . he said . . . he said . . . something about. . . he lived here.
MICK. Yes, he's got a point, en he?

DAVIES. A point! This is your house, en't? You let him live here!

MICK. I could tell him to go, I suppose.

DAVIES. That's what I'm saying.

MICK. Yes. I could tell him to go. I mean, I'm the landlord. On the other hand, he's the sitting tenant. Giving him notice, you see, what it is, it's a technical matter, that's what it is. It depends how you regard this room. I mean it depends whether you regard this room as furnished or un-furnished. See what I mean?

DAVIES. No, I don't.

MICK. All this furniture, you see, in here, it's all his, except the beds, of course. So what it is, it's a fine legal point, that's what it is.

Pause.

DAVIES. I tell you he should go back where he come from!

MICK (*turning to look at him*). Come from?

DAVIES. Yes.

MICK. Where did he come from?

DAVIES. Well . . . he . . . he. . . .

MICK. You get a bit out of your depth sometimes, don't you?
Pause.
(*Rising, briskly.*) Well, anyway, as things stand, I don't mind having a go at doing up the place. . . .

DAVIES. That's what I wanted to hear!

MICK. No, I don't mind.
He turns to face DAVIES.
But you better be as good as you say you are.

DAVIES. What do you mean?

MICK. Well, you say you're an interior decorator, you'd better be a good one.

DAVIES. A what?

MICK. What do you mean, a what? A decorator. An interior decorator.

DAVIES. Me? What do you mean? I never touched that. I never been that.

MICK. You've never what?

DAVIES. No, no, not me, man. I'm not an interior decorator. I been too busy. Too many other things to do, you see. But I . . . but I could always turn my hand to most things . . . give me . . . give me a bit of time to pick it up.

MICK. I don't want you to pick it up. I want a first-class experienced interior decorator. I thought you were one.

DAVIES. Me? Now wait a minute—wait a minute—you got the wrong man.

MICK. How could I have the wrong man? You're the only man I've spoken to. You're the only man I've told, about my dreams, about my deepest wishes, you're the only one I've told, and I only told you because I understood you were an experienced first-class professional interior and exterior decorator.

DAVIES. Now look here—

MICK. You mean you wouldn't know how to fit teal-blue, copper and parchment linoleum squares and have those colours re-echoed in the walls?

DAVIES. Now, look here, where'd you get—?

MICK. You wouldn't be able to decorate out a table in afromosia teak veneer, an armchair in oatmeal tweed and a beech frame settee with a woven sea-grass seat?

DAVIES. I never said that!

MICK. Christ! I must have been under a false impression!

DAVIES. I never said it!

MICK. You're a bloody impostor, mate!

DAVIES. Now you don't want to say that sort of thing to me. You took me on here as caretaker. I was going to give you a helping hand, that's all, for a small . . for a small wage, I never said nothing about that . . . you start calling me names—

MICK. What is your name?

DAVIES. Don't start that—

MICK. No, what's your real name?

DAVIES. My real name's Davies.

MICK. What's the name you go under?

DAVIES. Jenkins!

MICK. You got two names. What about the rest? Eh? Now come on, why did you tell me all this dirt about you being an interior decorator?

DAVIES. I didn't tell you nothing! Won't you listen to what I'm saying?

Pause.

It was him who told you. It was your brother who must have told you. He's nutty! He'd tell you anything, out of spite, he's nutty, he's half way gone, it was him who told you.

MICK *walks slowly to him.*

MICK. What did you call my brother?

DAVIES. When?

MICK. He's what?

DAVIES. I . . . now get this straight. . . .

MICK. Nutty? Who's nutty?

Pause.

Did you call my brother nutty? My brother. That's a bit of . . . . that's a bit of an impertinent thing to say, isn't it?

DAVIES. But he says so himself!

MICK *walks slowly round* DAVIES' *figure, regarding him, once. He circles him, once.*

MICK. What a strange man you are. Aren't you? You're really strange. Ever since you come into this house there's been nothing but trouble. Honest. I can take nothing you say at face value. Every word you speak is open to any number of different interpretations. Most of what you say is lies. You're violent, you're erratic, you're just completely unpredictable. You're nothing else but a wild animal, when you come down to it. You're a barbarian. And to put the old tin lid on it, you stink from arse-hole to breakfast time. Look at it. You come here recommending yourself as an interior decorator, where-upon I take you on, and what happens? You make a long speech about all the references you've got down at Sidcup, and what happens? I haven't noticed you go down to Sidcup to obtain them. It's all most regrettable but it looks as though I'm compelled to pay you off for your caretaking work. Here's half a dollar.

He feels in his pocket, takes out a half-crown and tosses it at DAVIES' *feet.* DAVIES *stands still.* MICK *walks to the gas stove and picks up the Buddha.*

DAVIES (*slowly*). All right then . . . you do that . . . you do it . . . if that's what you want. . . .

MICK. THAT'S WHAT I WANT!

He hurls the Buddha against the gas stove. It breaks.

(*Passionately.*) Anyone would think this house was all I got to worry about. I got plenty of other things I can worry about. I've got other things. I've got plenty of other interests. I've got my own business to build up, haven't I? I got to think about expanding . . . in all directions. I don't stand still. I'm moving about, all the time. I'm moving . . . all the time. I've got to think about the future. I'm not worried about this house. I'm not interested. My brother can worry about it. He can do it up, he can decorate it, he can do what he likes with it. I'm not bothered. I thought I was doing him a favour, letting him live here. He's got his own ideas. Let him have them. I'm going to chuck it in.

Pause.

DAVIES. What about me?

Silence. MICK *does not look at him.*
A door bangs.

Silence. They do not move.

ASTON *comes in. He closes the door, moves into the room and faces* MICK. *They look at each other. Both are smiling, faintly.*

MICK (*beginning to speak to* ASTON). Look... uh...

He stops, goes to the door and exits. ASTON *leaves the door open, crosses behind* DAVIES, *sees the broken Buddha, and looks at the pieces for a moment. He then goes to his bed, takes off his overcoat, sits, takes the screwdriver and plug and pokes the plug.*

DAVIES. I just come back for my pipe.

ASTON. Oh yes.

DAVIES. I got out and . . . half way down I . . . I suddenly . . . found out . . . you see . . . that I hadn't got my pipe. So I come back to get it. . . .

Pause. He moves to ASTON.

That ain't the same plug, is it, you been . . . ?

Pause.

Still can't get anywhere with it, eh?

Pause.

Well, if you . . . persevere, in my opinion, you'll probably . . .

Pause.

Listen. . . .

Pause.

You didn't mean that, did you, about me stinking, did you?

Pause.

Did you? You been a good friend to me. You took me in. You took me in, you didn't ask me no questions, you give me a bed, you been a mate to me. Listen. I been thinking, why I made all them noises, it was because of the draught, see, that draught was on me as I was sleeping, made me make noises without me knowing it, so I been thinking, what I mean to say, if you was to give me your bed, and you have

my bed, there's not all that difference between them, they're
the same sort of bed, if I was to have yourn, you sleep,
wherever bed you're in, so you have mine, I have yourn, and
that'll be all right, I'll be out of the draught, see, I mean,
you don't mind a bit of wind, you need a bit of air, I can
understand that, you being in that place that time, with all
them doctors and all they done, closed up, I know them
places, too hot, you see, they're always too hot, I had a peep
in one once, nearly suffocated me, so I reckon that'd be the
best way out of it, we swap beds, and then we could get down
to what we was saying, I'd look after the place for you, I'd
keep an eye on it for you, for you, like, not for the other . . .
not for . . . for your brother, you see, not for him, for you,
I'll be your man, you say the word, just say the word. . . .
    Pause.
What do you think of this I'm saying ?

    Pause.

ASTON. No, I like sleeping in this bed.
DAVIES. But you don't understand my meaning!
ASTON. Anyway, that one's my brother's bed.
DAVIES. Your brother ?
ASTON. Any time he stays here. This is my bed. It's the only
    bed I can sleep in.
DAVIES. But your brother's gone! He's gone!

    Pause.

ASTON. No. I couldn't change beds.
DAVIES. But you don't understand my meaning!
ASTON. Anyway, I'm going to be busy. I've got that shed to
    get up. If I don't get it up now it'll never go up. Until it's up
    I can't get started.
DAVIES. I'll give you a hand to put up your shed, that's what
    I'll do!
    Pause.

I'll give you a hand! We'll both put up that shed together!
See? Get it done in next to no time! Do you see what
I'm saying?

   Pause.

ASTON. No. I can get it up myself.
DAVIES. But listen. I'm with you, I'll be here, I'll do it for
you!
   Pause.
We'll do it together!
   Pause.
Christ, we'll change beds!
   ASTON *moves to the window and stands with his back to*
   DAVIES.
You mean you're throwing me out? You can't do that.
Listen man, listen man, I don't mind, you see, I don't mind,
I'll stay, I don't mind, I'll tell you what, if you don't want
to change beds, we'll keep it as it is, I'll stay in the same bed,
maybe if I can get a stronger piece of sacking, like, to go
over the window, keep out the draught, that'll do it, what do
you say, we'll keep it as it is?

   Pause.

ASTON. No.
DAVIES. Why . . . not?

   ASTON *turns to look at him.*

ASTON. You make too much noise.
DAVIES. But . . . but . . . look . . . listen . . . listen here . . .
I mean. . . .
   ASTON *turns back to the window.*
What am I going to do?
   Pause.
What shall I do?
   Pause.

Where am I going to go ?

Pause.

If you want me to go . . . I'll go. You just say the word.

Pause.

I'll tell you what though . . . them shoes . . . them shoes you give me . . . they're working out all right . . . they're all right. Maybe I could . . . get down. . . .

ASTON *remains still, his back to him, at the window.*

Listen . . . if I . . . got down . . . if I was to . . . get my papers . . . would you . . . would you let . . . would you . . . if I got down . . . and got my. . . .

Long silence.

Curtain.

The Dumb Waiter

THE DUMB WAITER was first presented at the Hampstead Theatre Club on 21st January, 1960, with the following cast:

BEN   Nicholas Selby
GUS   George Tovey

THE DUMB WAITER was subsequently presented at the Royal Court Theatre on 8th March, 1960, with the same cast.

Scene: A basement room. Two beds, flat against the back wall. A serving hatch, closed, between the beds. A door to the kitchen and lavatory, left. A door to a passage, right.

BEN *is lying on a bed, left, reading a paper.* GUS *is sitting on a bed, right, tying his shoelaces, with difficulty. Both are dressed in shirts, trousers and braces.*

Silence.

GUS *ties his laces, rises, yawns and begins to walk slowly to the door, left. He stops, looks down, and shakes his foot.*

BEN *lowers his paper and watches him.* GUS *kneels and unties his shoe-lace and slowly takes off the shoe. He looks inside it and brings out a flattened matchbox. He shakes it and examines it. Their eyes meet.* BEN *rattles his paper and reads.* GUS *puts the matchbox in his pocket and bends down to put on his shoe. He ties his lace, with difficulty.* BEN *lowers his paper and watches him.* GUS *walks to the door, left, stops, and shakes the other foot. He kneels, unties his shoe-lace, and slowly takes off the shoe. He looks inside it and brings out a flattened cigarette packet. He shakes it and examines it. Their eyes meet.* BEN *rattles his paper and reads.* GUS *puts the packet in his pocket, bends down, puts on his shoe and ties the lace.*

He wanders off, left.

BEN *slams the paper down on the bed and glares after him. He picks up the paper and lies on his back, reading.*

Silence.

A lavatory chain is pulled twice off, left, but the lavatory does not flush.

Silence.

GUS *re-enters, left, and halts at the door, scratching his head.* BEN *slams down the paper.*

BEN. Kaw!

He picks up the paper.

What about this? Listen to this!

He refers to the paper.

A man of eighty-seven wanted to cross the road. But there was a lot of traffic, see? He couldn't see how he was going to squeeze through. So he crawled under a lorry.

GUS. He what?

BEN. He crawled under a lorry. A stationary lorry.

GUS. No?

BEN. The lorry started and ran over him.

GUS. Go on!

BEN. That's what it says here.

GUS. Get away.

BEN. It's enough to make you want to puke, isn't it?

GUS. Who advised him to do a thing like that?

BEN. A man of eighty-seven crawling under a lorry!

GUS. It's unbelievable.

BEN. It's down here in black and white.

GUS. Incredible.

> *Silence.*
> GUS *shakes his head and exits.* BEN *lies back and reads.*
> *The lavatory chain is pulled once off left, but the lavatory does not flush.*
> BEN *whistles at an item in the paper.*
> GUS *re-enters.*

I want to ask you something.

BEN. What are you doing out there?

GUS. Well, I was just—

BEN. What about the tea?

GUS. I'm just going to make it.

BEN. Well, go on, make it.

GUS. Yes, I will. (*He sits in a chair. Ruminatively.*) He's laid on some very nice crockery this time, I'll say that. It's sort of striped. There's a white stripe.

BEN *reads*.

It's very nice. I'll say that.

BEN *turns the page*.

You know, sort of round the cup. Round the rim. All the rest of it's black, you see. Then the saucer's black, except for right in the middle, where the cup goes, where it's white.

BEN *reads*.

Then the plates are the same, you see. Only they've got a black stripe—the plates—right across the middle. Yes, I'm quite taken with the crockery.

BEN (*still reading*). What do you want plates for? You're not going to eat.

GUS. I've brought a few biscuits.

BEN. Well, you'd better eat them quick.

GUS. I always bring a few biscuits. Or a pie. You know I can't drink tea without anything to eat.

BEN. Well, make the tea then, will you? Time's getting on.

GUS *brings out the flattened cigarette packet and examines it.*

GUS. You got any cigarettes? I think I've run out.

He throws the packet high up and leans forward to catch it.

I hope it won't be a long job, this one.

Aiming carefully, he flips the packet under his bed.

Oh, I wanted to ask you something.

BEN (*slamming his paper down*). Kaw!

GUS. What's that?

BEN. A child of eight killed a cat!

GUS. Get away.

BEN. It's a fact. What about that, eh? A child of eight killing a cat!

GUS. How did he do it?

BEN. It was a girl.

GUS. How did she do it?

BEN. She—

He picks up the paper and studies it.

It doesn't say.

GUS. Why not?

BEN. Wait a minute. It just says—Her brother, aged eleven, viewed the incident from the toolshed.

GUS. Go on!

BEN. That's bloody ridiculous.

Pause.

GUS. I bet he did it.

BEN. Who?

GUS. The brother.

BEN. I think you're right.

Pause.

(*Slamming down the paper.*) What about that, eh? A kid of eleven killing a cat and blaming it on his little sister of eight! It's enough to—

He breaks off in disgust and seizes the paper. GUS *rises.*

GUS. What time is he getting in touch?

BEN *reads.*

What time is he getting in touch?

BEN. What's the matter with you? It could be any time. Any time.

GUS (*moves to the foot of* BEN'S *bed*). Well, I was going to ask you something.

BEN. What?

GUS. Have you noticed the time that tank takes to fill ?

BEN. What tank ?

GUS. In the lavatory.

BEN. No. Does it ?

GUS. Terrible.

BEN. Well, what about it ?

GUS. What do you think's the matter with it ?

BEN. Nothing.

GUS. Nothing ?

BEN. It's got a deficient ballcock, that's all.

GUS. A deficient what ?

BEN. Ballcock.

GUS. No ? Really ?

BEN. That's what I should say.

GUS. Go on! That didn't occur to me.

> GUS *wanders to his bed and presses the mattress.*

I didn't have a very restful sleep today, did you ? It's not much of a bed. I could have done with another blanket too. (*He catches sight of a picture on the wall.*) Hello, what's this ? (*Peering at it.*) "The First Eleven." Cricketers. You seen this, Ben ?

BEN (*reading*). What ?

GUS. The first eleven.

BEN. What ?

GUS. There's a photo here of the first eleven.

BEN. What first eleven ?

GUS (*studying the photo*). It doesn't say.

BEN. What about that tea ?

GUS. They all look a bit old to me.

> GUS *wanders downstage, looks out front, then all about the room.*

I wouldn't like to live in this dump. I wouldn't mind if you had a window, you could see what it looked like outside.

BEN. What do you want a window for?

GUS. Well, I like to have a bit of a view, Ben. It whiles away the time.

He walks about the room.

I mean, you come into a place when it's still dark, you come into a room you've never seen before, you sleep all day, you do your job, and then you go away in the night again.

Pause.

I like to get a look at the scenery. You never get the chance in this job.

BEN. You get your holidays, don't you?

GUS. Only a fortnight.

BEN (*lowering the paper*). You kill me. Anyone would think you're working every day. How often do we do a job? Once a week? What are you complaining about?

GUS. Yes, but we've got to be on tap though, haven't we? You can't move out of the house in case a call comes.

BEN. You know what your trouble is?

GUS. What?

BEN. You haven't got any interests.

GUS. I've got interests.

BEN. What? Tell me one of your interests.

Pause.

GUS. I've got interests.

BEN. Look at me. What have I got?

GUS. I don't know. What?

BEN. I've got my woodwork. I've got my model boats. Have you ever seen me idle? I'm never idle. I know how to occupy my time, to its best advantage. Then when a call comes, I'm ready.

GUS. Don't you ever get a bit fed up?

BEN. Fed up? What with?

Silence.

BEN *reads.* GUS *feels in the pocket of his jacket, which hangs on the bed.*

GUS. You got any cigarettes? I've run out.

The lavatory flushes off left.

There she goes.

GUS *sits on his bed.*

No, I mean, I say the crockery's good. It is. It's very nice. But that's about all I can say for this place. It's worse than the last one. Remember that last place we were in? Last time, where was it? At least there was a wireless there. No, honest. He doesn't seem to bother much about our comfort these days.

BEN. When are you going to stop jabbering?

GUS. You'd get rheumatism in a place like this, if you stay long.

BEN. We're not staying long. Make the tea, will you? We'll be on the job in a minute.

GUS *picks up a small bag by his bed and brings out a packet of tea. He examines it and looks up.*

GUS. Eh, I've been meaning to ask you.

BEN. What the hell is it now?

GUS. Why did you stop the car this morning, in the middle of that road?

BEN (*lowering the paper*). I thought you were asleep.

GUS. I was, but I woke up when you stopped. You did stop, didn't you?

Pause.

In the middle of that road. It was still dark, don't you remember? I looked out. It was all misty. I thought perhaps you wanted to kip, but you were sitting up dead straight, like you were waiting for something.

BEN. I wasn't waiting for anything.

GUS. I must have fallen asleep again. What was all that about then? Why did you stop?

BEN (*picking up the paper*). We were too early.

GUS. Early? (*He rises.*) What do you mean? We got the call, didn't we, saying we were to start right away. We did. We shoved out on the dot. So how could we be too early?

BEN (*quietly*). Who took the call, me or you?

GUS. You.

BEN. We were too early.

GUS. Too early for what?

Pause.

You mean someone had to get out before we got in?

He examines the bedclothes.

I thought these sheets didn't look too bright. I thought they ponged a bit. I was too tired to notice when I got in this morning. Eh, that's taking a bit of a liberty, isn't it? I don't want to share my bed-sheets. I told you things were going down the drain. I mean, we've always had clean sheets laid on up till now. I've noticed it.

BEN. How do you know those sheets weren't clean?

GUS. What do you mean?

BEN. How do you know they weren't clean? You've spent the whole day in them, haven't you?

GUS. What, you mean it might be my pong? (*He sniffs sheets.*) Yes. (*He sits slowly on bed.*) It could be my pong, I suppose. It's difficult to tell. I don't really know what I pong like, that's the trouble.

BEN (*referring to the paper*). Kaw!

GUS. Eh, Ben.

BEN. Kaw!

GUS. Ben.

BEN. What?

GUS. What town are we in? I've forgotten.

BEN. I've told you. Birmingham.

GUS. Go on!

He looks with interest about the room.

That's in the Midlands. The second biggest city in Great Britain. I'd never have guessed.

He snaps his fingers.

Eh, it's Friday today, isn't it? It'll be Saturday tomorrow.

BEN. What about it?

GUS (*excited*). We could go and watch the Villa.

BEN. They're playing away.

GUS. No, are they? Caarr! What a pity.

BEN. Anyway, there's no time. We've got to get straight back.

GUS. Well, we have done in the past, haven't we? Stayed over and watched a game, haven't we? For a bit of relaxation.

BEN. Things have tightened up, mate. They've tightened up.

GUS *chuckles to himself.*

GUS. I saw the Villa get beat in a cup tie once. Who was it against now? White shirts. It was one-all at half-time. I'll never forget it. Their opponents won by a penalty. Talk about drama. Yes, it was a disputed penalty. Disputed. They got beat two–one, anyway, because of it. You were there yourself.

BEN. Not me.

GUS. Yes, you were there. Don't you remember that disputed penalty?

BEN. No.

GUS. He went down just inside the area. Then they said he was just acting. I didn't think the other bloke touched him myself. But the referee had the ball on the spot.

BEN. Didn't touch him! What are you talking about? He laid him out flat!

GUS. Not the Villa. The Villa don't play that sort of game.

BEN. Get out of it.

   Pause.

GUS. Eh, that must have been here, in Birmingham.

BEN. What must?

GUS. The Villa. That must have been here.

BEN. They were playing away.

GUS. Because you know who the other team was? It was the Spurs. It was Tottenham Hotspur.

BEN. Well, what about it?

GUS. We've never done a job in Tottenham.

BEN. How do you know?

GUS. I'd remember Tottenham.

   BEN *turns on his bed to look at him.*

BEN. Don't make me laugh, will you?

   BEN *turns back and reads.* GUS *yawns and speaks through his yawn.*

GUS. When's he going to get in touch?

   Pause.

Yes, I'd like to see another football match. I've always been an ardent football fan. Here, what about coming to see the Spurs tomorrow?

BEN (*tonelessly*). They're playing away.

GUS. Who are?

BEN. The Spurs.

GUS. Then they might be playing here.

BEN. Don't be silly.

GUS. If they're playing away they might be playing here. They might be playing the Villa.

BEN (*tonelessly*). But the Villa are playing away.

   Pause. An envelope slides under the door, right. GUS *sees it. He stands, looking at it.*

GUS. Ben.

BEN. Away. They're all playing away.

GUS. Ben, look here.

BEN. What?

GUS. Look.

BEN *turns his head and sees the envelope. He stands.*

BEN. What's that?

GUS. I don't know.

BEN. Where did it come from?

GUS. Under the door.

BEN. Well, what is it?

GUS. I don't know.

They stare at it.

BEN. Pick it up.

GUS. What do you mean?

BEN. Pick it up!

GUS *slowly moves towards it, bends and picks it up.*

What is it?

GUS. An envelope.

BEN. Is there anything on it?

GUS. No.

BEN. Is it sealed?

GUS. Yes.

BEN. Open it.

GUS. What?

BEN. Open it!

GUS *opens it and looks inside.*

What's in it?

GUS *empties twelve matches into his hand.*

GUS. Matches.

BEN. Matches?
GUS. Yes.
BEN. Show it to me.

> GUS *passes the envelope.* BEN *examines it.*

Nothing on it. Not a word.
GUS. That's funny, isn't it?
BEN. It came under the door?
GUS. Must have done.
BEN. Well, go on.
GUS. Go on where?
BEN. Open the door and see if you can catch anyone outside.
GUS. Who, me?
BEN. Go on!

> GUS *stares at him, puts the matches in his pocket, goes to his bed and brings a revolver from under the pillow. He goes to the door, opens it, looks out and shuts it.*

GUS. No one.

> *He replaces the revolver.*

BEN. What did you see?
GUS. Nothing.
BEN. They must have been pretty quick.

> GUS *takes the matches from pocket and looks at them.*

GUS. Well, they'll come in handy.
BEN. Yes.
GUS. Won't they?
BEN. Yes, you're always running out, aren't you?
GUS. All the time.
BEN. Well, they'll come in handy then.
GUS. Yes.
BEN. Won't they?
GUS. Yes, I could do with them. I could do with them too.

BEN. You could, eh?

GUS. Yes.

BEN. Why?

GUS. We haven't got any.

BEN. Well, you've got some now, haven't you?

GUS. I can light the kettle now.

BEN. Yes, you're always cadging matches. How many have you got there?

GUS. About a dozen.

BEN. Well, don't lose them. Red too. You don't even need a box.

> GUS *probes his ear with a match.*

(*Slapping his hand*). Don't waste them! Go on, go and light it.

GUS. Eh?

BEN. Go and light it.

GUS. Light what?

BEN. The kettle.

GUS. You mean the gas.

BEN. Who does?

GUS. You do.

BEN (*his eyes narrowing*). What do you mean, I mean the gas?

GUS. Well, that's what you mean, don't you? The gas.

BEN (*powerfully*). If I say go and light the kettle I mean go and light the kettle.

GUS. How can you light a kettle?

BEN. It's a figure of speech! Light the kettle. It's a figure of speech!

GUS. I've never heard it.

BEN. Light the kettle! It's common usage!

GUS. I think you've got it wrong.

BEN (*menacing*). What do you mean?

GUS. They say put on the kettle.

BEN (*taut*). Who says?

> *They stare at each other, breathing hard.*

(*Deliberately.*) I have never in all my life heard anyone say put on the kettle.

GUS. I bet my mother used to say it.

BEN. Your mother? When did you last see your mother?

GUS. I don't know, about—

BEN. Well, what are you talking about your mother for?

They stare.

Gus, I'm not trying to be unreasonable. I'm just trying to point out something to you.

GUS. Yes, but—

BEN. Who's the senior partner here, me or you?

GUS. You.

BEN. I'm only looking after your interests, Gus. You've got to learn, mate.

GUS. Yes, but I've never heard—

BEN (*vehemently*). Nobody says light the gas! What does the gas light?

GUS. What does the gas—?

BEN (*grabbing him with two hands by the throat, at arm's length*). THE KETTLE, YOU FOOL!

GUS *takes the hands from his throat.*

GUS. All right, all right.

Pause.

BEN. Well, what are you waiting for?

GUS. I want to see if they light.

BEN. What?

GUS. The matches.

He takes out the flattened box and tries to strike.

No.

He throws the box under the bed.
BEN *stares at him.*

GUS *raises his foot.*

Shall I try it on here?

BEN *stares.* GUS *strikes a match on his shoe. It lights.*

Here we are.

BEN (*wearily*). Put on the bloody kettle, for Christ's sake.

BEN *goes to his bed, but, realising what he has said, stops and half turns. They look at each other.* GUS *slowly exits, left.* BEN *slams his paper down on the bed and sits on it, head in hands.*

GUS (*entering*). It's going.

BEN. What?

GUS. The stove.

GUS *goes to his bed and sits.*

I wonder who it'll be tonight.

Silence.

Eh, I've been wanting to ask you something.

BEN (*putting his legs on the bed*). Oh, for Christ's sake.

GUS. No. I was going to ask you something.

He rises and sits on BEN'S *bed.*

BEN. What are you sitting on my bed for?

GUS *sits.*

What's the matter with you? You're always asking me questions. What's the matter with you?

GUS. Nothing.

BEN. You never used to ask me so many damn questions. What's come over you?

GUS. No, I was just wondering.

BEN. Stop wondering. You've got a job to do. Why don't you just do it and shut up?

GUS. That's what I was wondering about.

BEN. What?

GUS. The job.

BEN. What job?

GUS (*tentatively*). I thought perhaps you might know something.

> BEN *looks at him.*

I thought perhaps you—I mean—have you got any idea—who it's going to be tonight?

BEN. Who what's going to be?

> *They look at each other.*

GUS (*at length*). Who it's going to be.

> *Silence.*

BEN. Are you feeling all right?

GUS. Sure.

BEN. Go and make the tea.

GUS. Yes, sure.

> GUS *exits, left,* BEN *looks after him. He then takes his revolver from under the pillow and checks it for ammunition.* GUS *re-enters.*

The gas has gone out.

BEN. Well, what about it?

GUS. There's a meter.

BEN. I haven't got any money.

GUS. Nor have I.

BEN. You'll have to wait.

GUS. What for?

BEN. For Wilson.

GUS. He might not come. He might just send a message. He doesn't always come.

BEN. Well, you'll have to do without it, won't you?

GUS. Blimey.

BEN. You'll have a cup of tea afterwards. What's the matter with you?

GUS. I like to have one before.

BEN *holds the revolver up to the light and polishes it.*

BEN. You'd better get ready anyway.

GUS. Well, I don't know, that's a bit much, you know, for my money.

He picks up a packet of tea from the bed and throws it into the bag.

I hope he's got a shilling, anyway, if he comes. He's entitled to have. After all, it's his place, he could have seen there was enough gas for a cup of tea.

BEN. What do you mean, it's his place?

GUS. Well, isn't it?

BEN. He's probably only rented it. It doesn't have to be his place.

GUS. I know it's his place. I bet the whole house is. He's not even laying on any gas now either.

GUS *sits on his bed.*

It's his place all right. Look at all the other places. You go to this address, there's a key there, there's a teapot, there's never a soul in sight—(*He pauses.*) Eh, nobody ever hears a thing, have you ever thought of that? We never get any complaints, do we, too much noise or anything like that? You never see a soul, do you?—except the bloke who comes. You ever noticed that? I wonder if the walls are sound-proof. (*He touches the wall above his bed.*) Can't tell. All you do is wait, eh? Half the time he doesn't even bother to put in an appearance, Wilson.

BEN. Why should he? He's a busy man.

GUS (*thoughtfully*). I find him hard to talk to, Wilson. Do you know that, Ben?

BEN. Scrub round it, will you?

Pause.

GUS. There are a number of things I want to ask him. But I can never get round to it, when I see him.

Pause.

I've been thinking about the last one.
BEN. What last one?
GUS. That girl.

BEN *grabs the paper, which he reads.*

(*Rising, looking down at* BEN). How many times have you read that paper?

BEN *slams the paper down and rises.*

BEN (*angrily*). What do you mean?
GUS. I was just wondering how many times you'd—
BEN. What are you doing, criticising me?
GUS. No, I was just—
BEN. You'll get a swipe round your earhole if you don't watch your step.
GUS. Now look here, Ben—
BEN. I'm not looking anywhere! (*He addresses the room.*) How many times have I—! A bloody liberty!
GUS. I didn't mean that.
BEN. You just get on with it, mate. Get on with it, that's all.

BEN *gets back on the bed.*

GUS. I was just thinking about that girl, that's all.

GUS *sits on his bed.*

She wasn't much to look at, I know, but still. It was a mess though, wasn't it? What a mess. Honest, I can't remember a mess like that one. They don't seem to hold together like

men, women. A looser texture, like. Didn't she spread, eh ?
She didn't half spread. Kaw! But I've been meaning to ask
you.

BEN *sits up and clenches his eyes.*

Who clears up after we've gone ? I'm curious about that.
Who does the clearing up ? Maybe they don't clear up.
Maybe they just leave them there, eh ? What do you think ?
How many jobs have we done ? Blimey, I can't count them.
What if they never clear anything up after we've gone.

BEN (*pityingly*). You mutt. Do you think we're the only
branch of this organisation ? Have a bit of common. They
got departments for everything.

GUS. What cleaners and all ?

BEN. You birk!

GUS. No, it was that girl made me start to think—

*There is a loud clatter and racket in the bulge of wall between
the beds, of something descending. They grab their revolvers,
jump up and face the wall. The noise comes to a stop. Silence.
They look at each other. BEN gestures sharply towards the
wall. GUS approaches the wall slowly. He bangs it with his
revolver. It is hollow. BEN moves to the head of his bed, his
revolver cocked. GUS puts his revolver on his bed and pats
along the bottom of the centre panel. He finds a rim. He lifts
the panel. Disclosed is a serving-hatch, a "dumb waiter". A
wide box is held by pulleys. GUS peers into the box. He brings
out a piece of paper.*

BEN. What is it ?

GUS. You have a look at it.

BEN. Read it.

GUS (*reading*). Two braised steak and chips. Two sago pud-
dings. Two teas without sugar.

BEN. Let me see that. (*He takes the paper.*)

GUS (*to himself*). Two teas without sugar.

BEN. Mmnn.

GUS. What do you think of that?

BEN. Well—

The box goes up. BEN *levels his revolver.*

GUS. Give us a chance! They're in a hurry, aren't they?

BEN *re-reads the note.* GUS *looks over his shoulder.*

That's a bit—that's a bit funny, isn't it?

BEN (*quickly*). No. It's not funny. It probably used to be a café here, that's all. Upstairs. These places change hands very quickly.

GUS. A café?

BEN. Yes.

GUS. What, you mean this was the kitchen, down here?

BEN. Yes, they change hands overnight, these places. Go into liquidation. The people who run it, you know, they don't find it a going concern, they move out.

GUS. You mean the people who ran this place didn't find it a going concern and moved out?

BEN. Sure.

GUS. WELL, WHO'S GOT IT NOW?

Silence.

BEN. What do you mean, who's got it now?

GUS. Who's got it now? If they moved out, who moved in?

BEN. Well, that all depends—

The box descends with a clatter and bang. BEN *levels his revolver.* GUS *goes to the box and brings out a piece of paper.*

GUS (*reading*). Soup of the day. Liver and onions. Jam tart.

A pause. GUS *looks at* BEN. BEN *takes the note and reads it. He walks slowly to the hatch.* GUS *follows.* BEN *looks into the hatch but not up it.* GUS *puts his hand on* BEN'S *shoulder.* BEN *throws it off.* GUS *puts his finger to his mouth. He leans on the hatch and swiftly looks up it.* BEN *flings him away in alarm.* BEN *looks at the note. He throws his revolver on the bed and speaks with decision.*

BEN. We'd better send something up.
GUS. Eh?
BEN. We'd better send something up.
GUS. Oh! Yes. Yes. Maybe you're right.

> *They are both relieved at the decision.*

BEN (*purposefully*). Quick! What have you got in that bag?
GUS. Not much.

> GUS *goes to the hatch and shouts up it.*

Wait a minute!
BEN. Don't do that!

> GUS *examines the contents of the bag and brings them out, one by one.*

GUS. Biscuits. A bar of chocolate. Half a pint of milk.
BEN. That all?
GUS. Packet of tea.
BEN. Good.
GUS. We can't send the tea. That's all the tea we've got.
BEN. Well, there's no gas. You can't do anything with it, can you?
GUS. Maybe they can send us down a bob.
BEN. What else is there?
GUS (*reaching into bag*). One Eccles cake.
BEN. One Eccles cake?
GUS. Yes.
BEN. You never told me you had an Eccles cake.
GUS. Didn't I?
BEN. Why only one? Didn't you bring one for me?
GUS. I didn't think you'd be keen.
BEN. Well, you can't send up one Eccles cake, anyway.

GUS. Why not?

BEN. Fetch one of those plates.

GUS. All right.

> GUS *goes towards the door, left, and stops.*

Do you mean I can keep the Eccles cake then?

BEN. Keep it?

GUS. Well, they don't know we've got it, do they?

BEN. That's not the point.

GUS. Can't I keep it?

BEN. No, you can't. Get the plate.

> GUS *exits, left.* BEN *looks in the bag. He brings out a packet of crisps. Enter* GUS *with a plate.*

(*Accusingly, holding up the crisps*). Where did these come from?

GUS. What?

BEN. Where did these crisps come from?

GUS. Where did you find them?

BEN (*hitting him on the shoulder*). You're playing a dirty game, my lad!

GUS. I only eat those with beer!

BEN. Well, where were you going to get the beer?

GUS. I was saving them till I did.

BEN. I'll remember this. Put everything on the plate.

> *They pile everything on to the plate. The box goes up without the plate.*

Wait a minute!

> *They stand.*

GUS. It's gone up.

BEN. It's all your stupid fault, playing about!

GUS. What do we do now?

BEN. We'll have to wait till it comes down.

BEN *puts the plate on the bed, puts on his shoulder holster,
and starts to put on his tie.*

You'd better get ready.

GUS *goes to his bed, puts on his tie, and starts to fix his
holster.*

GUS. Hey, Ben.
BEN. What?
GUS. What's going on here?

Pause.

BEN. What do you mean?
GUS. How can this be a café?
BEN. It used to be a café.
GUS. Have you seen the gas stove?
BEN. What about it?
GUS. It's only got three rings.
BEN. So what?
GUS. Well, you couldn't cook much on three rings, not for a
busy place like this.
BEN (*irritably*). That's why the service is slow!

BEN *puts on his waistcoat.*

GUS. Yes, but what happens when we're not here? What do
they do then? All these menus coming down and nothing
going up. It might have been going on like this for years.

BEN *brushes his jacket.*

What happens when we go?

BEN *puts on his jacket.*

They can't do much business.

The box descends. They turn about. GUS *goes to the hatch and
brings out a note.*

GUS (*reading*). Macaroni Pastitsio. Ormitha Macarounada.

BEN. What was that?

GUS. Macaroni Pastitsio. Ormitha Macarounada.

BEN. Greek dishes.

GUS. No.

BEN. That's right.

GUS. That's pretty high class.

BEN. Quick before it goes up.

> GUS *puts the plate in the box.*

GUS (*calling up the hatch*). Three McVitie and Price! One Lyons Red Label! One Smith's Crisps! One Eccles cake! One Fruit and Nut!

BEN. Cadbury's.

GUS (*up the hatch*). Cadbury's!

BEN (*handing the milk*). One bottle of milk.

GUS (*up the hatch*). One bottle of milk! Half a pint! (*He looks at the label.*) Express Dairy! (*He puts the bottle in the box.*)

> *The box goes up.*

Just did it.

BEN. You shouldn't shout like that.

GUS. Why not?

BEN. It isn't done.

> BEN *goes to his bed.*

Well, that should be all right, anyway, for the time being.

GUS. You think so, eh?

BEN. Get dressed, will you? It'll be any minute now.

> GUS *puts on his waistcoat.* BEN *lies down and looks up at the ceiling.*

GUS. This is some place. No tea and no biscuits.

BEN. Eating makes you lazy, mate. You're getting lazy, you know that? You don't want to get slack on your job.

GUS. Who me?

BEN. Slack, mate, slack.

GUS. Who me? Slack?

BEN. Have you checked your gun? You haven't even checked your gun. It looks disgraceful, anyway. Why don't you ever polish it?

> GUS *rubs his revolver on the sheet.* BEN *takes out a pocket mirror and straightens his tie.*

GUS. I wonder where the cook is. They must have had a few, to cope with that. Maybe they had a few more gas stoves. Eh! Maybe there's another kitchen along the passage.

BEN. Of course there is! Do you know what it takes to make an Ormitha Macarounada?

GUS. No, what?

BEN. An Ormitha—! Buck your ideas up, will you?

GUS. Takes a few cooks, eh?

> GUS *puts his revolver in its holster.*

The sooner we're out of this place the better.

> *He puts on his jacket.*

Why doesn't he get in touch? I feel like I've been here years. (*He takes his revolver out of its holster to check the ammunition.*) We've never let him down though, have we? We've never let him down. I was thinking only the other day, Ben. We're reliable, aren't we?

> *He puts his revolver back in its holster.*

Still, I'll be glad when it's over tonight.

> *He brushes his jacket.*

I hope the bloke's not going to get excited tonight, or anything. I'm feeling a bit off. I've got a splitting headache.

> *Silence.*

The box descends. BEN *jumps up.*
GUS *collects the note.*

(*Reading.*) One Bamboo Shoots, Water Chestnuts and Chicken. One Char Siu and Beansprouts.

BEN. Beansprouts?

GUS. Yes.

BEN. Blimey.

GUS. I wouldn't know where to begin.

He looks back at the box. The packet of tea is inside it. He picks it up.

They've sent back the tea.

BEN (*anxious*). What'd they do that for?

GUS. Maybe it isn't tea-time.

The box goes up. Silence.

BEN (*throwing the tea on the bed, and speaking urgently*). Look here. We'd better tell them.

GUS. Tell them what?

BEN. That we can't do it, we haven't got it.

GUS. All right then.

BEN. Lend us your pencil. We'll write a note.

GUS, *turning for a pencil, suddenly discovers the speaking-tube, which hangs on the right wall of the hatch facing his bed.*

GUS. What's this?

BEN. What?

GUS. This.

BEN (*examining it*). This? It's a speaking-tube.

GUS. How long has that been there?

BEN. Just the job. We should have used it before, instead of shouting up there.

GUS. Funny I never noticed it before.

BEN. Well, come on.

GUS. What do you do?

BEN. See that? That's a whistle.
GUS. What, this?
BEN. Yes, take it out. Pull it out.

GUS *does so.*

That's it.
GUS. What do we do now?
BEN. Blow into it.
GUS. Blow?
BEN. It whistles up there if you blow. Then they know you
want to speak. Blow.

GUS *blows. Silence.*

GUS (*tube at mouth*). I can't hear a thing.
BEN. Now you speak! Speak into it!

GUS *looks at* BEN, *then speaks into the tube.*

GUS. The larder's bare!
BEN. Give me that!

He grabs the tube and puts it to his mouth.

(*Speaking with great deference.*) Good evening. I'm sorry to
—bother you, but we just thought we'd better let you know
that we haven't got anything left. We sent up all we had.
There's no more food down here.

He brings the tube slowly to his ear.

What?

To mouth.

What?

To ear. He listens. To mouth.

No, all we had we sent up.

To ear. He listens. To mouth.

Oh, I'm very sorry to hear that.

To ear. He listens. To GUS.

The Eccles cake was stale.

He listens. To GUS.

The chocolate was melted.

He listens. To GUS.

The milk was sour.
GUS. What about the crisps?
BEN (*listening*). The biscuits were mouldy.

He glares at GUS. *Tube to mouth.*

Well, we're very sorry about that.

Tube to ear.

What?

To mouth.

What?

To ear.

Yes. Yes.

To mouth.

Yes certainly. Certainly. Right away.

To ear. The voice has ceased. He hangs up the tube.

(*Excitedly*). Did you hear that?

GUS. What?
BEN. You know what he said? Light the kettle! Not put on the
kettle! Not light the gas! But light the kettle!
GUS. How can we light the kettle?
BEN. What do you mean?

GUS. There's no gas.

BEN (*clapping hand to head*). Now what do we do?

GUS. What did he want us to light the kettle for?

BEN. For tea. He wanted a cup of tea.

GUS. *He* wanted a cup of tea! What about me? I've been wanting a cup of tea all night!

BEN (*despairingly*). What do we do now?

GUS. What are we supposed to drink?

> BEN *sits on his bed, staring.*

What about us?

> BEN *sits.*

I'm thirsty too. I'm starving. And he wants a cup of tea. That beats the band, that does.

> BEN *lets his head sink on to his chest.*

I could do with a bit of sustenance myself. What about you? You look as if you could do with something too.

> GUS *sits on his bed.*

We send him up all we've got and he's not satisfied. No, honest, it's enough to make the cat laugh. Why did you send him up all that stuff? (*Thoughtfully.*) Why did I send it up?

> *Pause.*

Who knows what he's got upstairs? He's probably got a salad bowl. They must have something up there. They won't get much from down here. You notice they didn't ask for any salads? They've probably got a salad bowl up there. Cold meat, radishes, cucumbers. Watercress. Roll mops.

> *Pause.*

Hardboiled eggs.

> *Pause.*

The lot. They've probably got a crate of beer too. Probably eating my crisps with a pint of beer now. Didn't have anything to say about those crisps, did he? They do all right, don't worry about that. You don't think they're just going to sit there and wait for stuff to come up from down here, do you? That'll get them nowhere.

Pause.

They do all right.

Pause.

And he wants a cup of tea.

Pause.

That's past a joke, in my opinion.

He looks over at BEN, *rises, and goes to him.*

What's the matter with you? You don't look too bright. I feel like an Alka-Seltzer myself.

BEN *sits up.*

BEN (*in a low voice*). Time's getting on.
GUS. I know. I don't like doing a job on an empty stomach.
BEN (*wearily*). Be quiet a minute. Let me give you your instructions.
GUS. What for? We always do it the same way, don't we?
BEN. Let me give you your instructions.

GUS *sighs and sits next to* BEN *on the bed. The instructions are stated and repeated automatically.*

When we get the call, you go over and stand behind the door.
GUS. Stand behind the door.
BEN. If there's a knock on the door you don't answer it.
GUS. If there's a knock on the door I don't answer it.
BEN. But there won't be a knock on the door.

GUS. So I won't answer it.
BEN. When the bloke comes in—
GUS. When the bloke comes in—
BEN. Shut the door behind him.
GUS. Shut the door behind him.
BEN. Without divulging your presence.
GUS. Without divulging my presence.
BEN. He'll see me and come towards me.
GUS. He'll see you and come towards you.
BEN. He won't see you.
GUS (*absently*). Eh?
BEN. He won't see you.
GUS. He won't see me.
BEN. But he'll see me.
GUS. He'll see you.
BEN. He won't know you're there.
GUS. He won't know you're there.
BEN. He won't know *you're* there.
GUS. He won't know I'm there.
BEN. I take out my gun.
GUS. You take out your gun.
BEN. He stops in his tracks.
GUS. He stops in his tracks.
BEN. If he turns round—
GUS. If he turns round—
BEN. You're there.
GUS. I'm here.

     BEN *frowns and presses his forehead.*

  You've missed something out.
BEN. I know. What?
GUS. I haven't taken my gun out, according to you.
BEN. You take your gun out—
GUS. After I've closed the door.
BEN. After you've closed the door.

GUS. You've never missed that out before, you know that?

BEN. When he sees you behind him—

GUS. Me behind him—

BEN. And me in front of him—

GUS. And you in front of him—

BEN. He'll feel uncertain—

GUS. Uneasy.

BEN. He won't know what to do.

GUS. So what will he do?

BEN. He'll look at me and he'll look at you.

GUS. We won't say a word.

BEN. We'll look at him.

GUS. He won't say a word.

BEN. He'll look at us.

GUS. And we'll look at him.

BEN. Nobody says a word.

Pause.

GUS. What do we do if it's a girl?

BEN. We do the same.

GUS. Exactly the same?

BEN. Exactly.

Pause.

GUS. We don't do anything different?

BEN. We do exactly the same.

GUS. Oh.

GUS *rises, and shivers.*

Excuse me.

He exits through the door on the left. BEN *remains sitting on the bed, still.*
The lavatory chain is pulled once off left, but the lavatory does not flush.
Silence.

GUS *re-enters and stops inside the door, deep in thought. He looks at* BEN, *then walks slowly across to his own bed. He is troubled. He stands, thinking. He turns and looks at* BEN. *He moves a few paces towards him.*

(*Slowly in a low, tense voice.*) Why did he send us matches if he knew there was no gas ?

Silence.

BEN *stares in front of him.* GUS *crosses to the left side of* BEN, *to the foot of his bed, to get to his other ear.*

Ben. Why did he send us matches if he knew there was no gas ?

BEN *looks up.*

Why did he do that ?

BEN. Who ?

GUS. Who sent us those matches ?

BEN. What are you talking about ?·

GUS *stares down at him.*

GUS (*thickly*). Who is it upstairs ?

BEN (*nervously*). What's one thing to do with another ?

GUS. Who is it, though ?

BEN. What's one thing to do with another ?

BEN *fumbles for his paper on the bed.*

GUS. I asked you a question.

BEN. Enough !

GUS (*with growing agitation*). I asked you before. Who moved in ? I asked you. You said the people who had it before moved out. Well, who moved in ?

BEN (*hunched*). Shut up.

GUS. I told you, didn't I ?

BEN (*standing*). Shut up !

GUS (*feverishly*). I told you before who owned this place, didn't I? I told you.

BEN *hits him viciously on the shoulder.*

I told you who ran this place, didn't I?

BEN *hits him viciously on the shoulder.*

(*Violently.*) Well, what's he playing all these games for? That's what I want to know. What's he doing it for?

BEN. What games?

GUS (*passionately, advancing*). What's he doing it for? We've been through our tests, haven't we? We got right through our tests, years ago, didn't we? We took them together, don't you remember, didn't we? We've proved ourselves before now, haven't we? We've always done our job. What's he doing all this for? What's the idea? What's he playing these games for?

The box in the shaft comes down behind them. The noise is this time accompanied by a shrill whistle, as it falls. GUS *rushes to the hatch and seizes the note.*

(*Reading.*) Scampi!

He crumples the note, picks up the tube, takes out the whistle, blows and speaks.

WE'VE GOT NOTHING LEFT! NOTHING! DO YOU UNDERSTAND?

BEN *seizes the tube and flings* GUS *away. He follows* GUS *and slaps him hard, back-handed, across the chest.*

BEN. Stop it! You maniac!

GUS. But you heard!

BEN (*savagely*). That's enough! I'm warning you!

Silence.

BEN *hangs the tube. He goes to his bed and lies down. He picks up his paper and reads.*

Silence.
The box goes up.
They turn quickly, their eyes meet. BEN *turns to his paper.*
Slowly GUS *goes back to his bed, and sits.*
Silence.
The hatch falls back into place.
They turn quickly, their eyes meet. BEN *turns back to his paper.*
Silence.
BEN *throws his paper down.*

BEN. Kaw!

He picks up the paper and looks at it.

Listen to this!

Pause.

What about that, eh?

Pause.

Kaw!

Pause.

Have you ever heard such a thing?
GUS (*dully*). Go on!
BEN. It's true.
GUS. Get away.
BEN. It's down here in black and white.
GUS (*very low*). Is that a fact?
BEN. Can you imagine it.
GUS. It's unbelievable.
BEN. It's enough to make you want to puke, isn't it?
GUS (*almost inaudible*). Incredible.

BEN *shakes his head. He puts the paper down and rises. He fixes the revolver in his holster.*

GUS stands up. He goes towards the door on the left.

BEN. Where are you going?

GUS. I'm going to have a glass of water.

He exits. BEN *brushes dust off his clothes and shoes. The whistle in the speaking-tube blows. He goes to it, takes the whistle out and puts the tube to his ear. He listens. He puts it to his mouth.*

BEN. Yes.

To ear. He listens. To mouth.

Straight away. Right.

To ear. He listens. To mouth.

Sure we're ready.

To ear. He listens. To mouth.

Understood. Repeat. He has arrived and will be coming in straight away. The normal method to be employed. Understood.

To ear. He listens. To mouth.

Sure we're ready.

To ear. He listens. To mouth.

Right.

He hangs the tube up.

Gus!

He takes out a comb and combs his hair, adjusts his jacket to diminish the bulge of the revolver. The lavatory flushes off left. BEN *goes quickly to the door, left.*

Gus!

The door right opens sharply. BEN *turns, his revolver levelled
at the door.*

GUS *stumbles in.*

*He is stripped of his jacket, waistcoat, tie, holster and
revolver.*

He stops, body stooping, his arms at his sides.

He raises his head and looks at BEN.

A long silence.

They stare at each other.

Curtain

A List of Evergreen Books

E4   **COUNT D'ORGEL** — Radiguet — $1.75
E6   **THE MARQUIS DE SADE** — Beauvoir — $1.95
E9   **JAPANESE LITERATURE** — Keene — $1.45
E23   **OEDIPUS: MYTH & COMPLEX** — Mullahy — $2.45
E25   **PUDD'NHEAD WILSON** — Twain — $1.45
E29   **POEMS OF CATULLUS** — Gregory — $1.95
E30   **THREE EXEMPLARY NOVELS** — Unamuno — $1.95
E31   **DEMOCRACY & DICTATORSHIP** — Barbu — $2.95
E33   **WAITING FOR GODOT** — Beckett — $1.75
E41   **THE PIT** — Norris — $2.95
E42   **THREEPENNY NOVEL** — Brecht — $2.95
E43   **WHITE JACKET** — Melville — $1.95
E44   **THE MAIDS AND DEATHWATCH** — Genet — $1.95
E47   **THE FORGOTTEN LANGUAGE** — Fromm — $1.75
E50   **PROUST** — Beckett — $1.45
E54   **POET IN NEW YORK** — Lorca — $1.95
E55   **PIERRE** — Melville — $2.95
E62   **THE NO PLAYS OF JAPAN** — Waley — $1.95
E67   **PSYCHOANALYSIS: EVOLUTION & DEVELOPMENT** — Thompson & Mullahy — $1.95
E71   **SELECTED POEMS OF H. D.** — $1.95
E90   **THREE PLAYS** — Ugo Betti — $2.45
E96   **ENDGAME** — Beckett — $1.45
E97   **THE ENDURING ART OF JAPAN** — Warner — $1.95
E101   **FOUR PLAYS** — Ionesco — $1.95
E104   **MURPHY** — Beckett — $1.95
E105   **SCIENCE OF CULTURE** — White — $2.95
E108   **WALKER IN THE CITY** — Kazin — $1.95
E112   **MONKEY** — Wu Ch'eng-en — $2.45
E119   **AMEDEE, THE NEW TENANT, VICTIMS OF DUTY** — Ionesco — $1.95
E124   **LOVES OF KRISHNA** — Archer — $1.95
E127   **THE THEATER AND ITS DOUBLE** — Artaud — $1.95
E130   **THE BALCONY** — Genet — $1.95
E139   **PSYCHOLOGY OF PERSONALITY** — McCarey, ed. — $2.95
E142   **WORLD OF WILLIAM FAULKNER** — Miner — $1.95
E143   **ALBERT CAMUS** — Thody — $1.45
E144   **FADE OUT** — Woolf — $1.75
E145   **WONDER THAT WAS INDIA** — Basham — $4.95
E152   **WATT** — Beckett — $2.45
E155   **THE KABUKI THEATRE** — Ernst — $3.95
E159   **A TASTE OF HONEY** — Delaney — $1.45
E163   **THE MONK** — Lewis — $2.45
E175   **ONE THOUSAND SOULS** — Pisemsky — $2.95
E180   **ESSAYS IN INDIVIDUAL PSYCHOLOGY** — Adler & Deutsch, eds. — $2.95
E181   **MARK TOBEY** — Roberts — $1.95
E187   **SELECTED POEMS OF BERTOLT BRECHT** — Hays, trans. — $1.95
E189   **THE KILLER** — Ionesco — $1.95
E190   **100 SELECTED POEMS OF E. E. CUMMINGS** — $1.75
E196   **PHILIP GUSTON** — Ashton — $1.95
E199   **STUART DAVIS** — Blesh — $1.95
E206   **RIVERS IN THE DESERT** — Glueck — $3.95
E208   **THE BLACKS** — Genet — $1.95

E216 **ANTHOLOGY OF JAPANESE LITERATURE** — Keene, ed. — $2.95
E219 **THE SPIRIT OF ZEN** — Watts — $1.75
E221 **ARTISTS' THEATRE** — Machiz, ed. — $2.45
E223 **THE CONNECTION** — Gelber — $1.75
E224 **CREATIVE VISION** — Block & Salinger, eds. — $2.45
E226 **KRAPP'S LAST TAPE** — Beckett — $1.95
E231 **MANUAL OF ZEN BUDDHISM** — Suzuki — $1.95
E237 **THE NEW AMERICAN POETRY** — Allen, ed. — $2.95
E240 **MODERN JAPANESE LITERATURE** — Keene, ed. — $2.45
E242 **DYNAMICS IN PSYCHOLOGY** — Kohler — $1.75
E253 **NADJA** — Breton — $1.95
E259 **RHINOCEROS** — Ionesco — $1.95
E268 **LITERARY LANDFALLS** — Aury — $1.95
E269 **KILLACHTER MEADOW** — Higgins — $1.95
E281 **MONSIEUR LEVERT** — Pinget — $1.95
E284 **HIROSHIMA MON AMOUR** — Duras — $1.95
E285 **CONTEMPORARY EUROPEAN PSYCHIATRY** — Bellak, ed. — $3.95
E286 **THE SOCIOLOGICAL IMAGINATION** — Mills — $1.95
E289 **ANTHOLOGY OF ZEN** — Briggs, ed. — $2.95
E291 **THE APPLE** — Gelber — $1.75
E297 **BAAL BABYLON** — Arrabal — $1.75
E299 **THE CARETAKER & THE DUMB WAITER** — Pinter — $1.75
E300 **TRANSACTIONAL ANALYSIS IN PSYCHOTHERAPY** — Berne — $3.95
E304 **THE DYING GLADIATORS** — Gregory — $2.45
E305 **THE WAY TO COLONOS** — Cicellis — $1.95
E307 **RED EYE OF LOVE** — Weinstein — $1.75
E309 **ESSAYS IN ZEN BUDDHISM** — Suzuki — $2.95
E310 **PROBLEMS OF HISTORICAL PSYCHOLOGY** — Barbu — $1.95
E312 **SERJEANT MUSGRAVE'S DANCE** — Arden — $1.75
E315 **THE BIRTHDAY PARTY & THE ROOM** — Pinter — $1.75
E317 **F'INGS AIN'T WOT THEY USED TO BE** — Norman — $1.75
E318 **HAPPY DAYS** — Beckett — $1.45
E320 **LAST YEAR AT MARIENBAD** — Robbe-Grillet — $1.95
E324 **THE FUTURE AS HISTORY** — Heilbroner — $1.75
E325 **ONE WAY PENDULUM** — Simpson — $1.75
E326 **THANK YOU AND OTHER POEMS** — Koch — $1.95
E327 **DOCK BRIEF AND OTHER PLAYS** — Mortimer — $1.95
E328 **THE PALM-WINE DRINKARD** — Tutuola — $1.45
E330 **WHAT THE BUDDHA TAUGHT** — Rahula — $1.75
E332 **MUNTU: AN OUTLINE OF THE NEW AFRICAN CULTURE** — Jahn — $2.45
E333 **BID ME TO LIVE** — H. D. — $1.95
E334 **MODERN GERMAN DRAMA** — Garten — $2.45
E338 **THE LION IN LOVE** — Delaney — $1.75
E344 **THE VISIT** — Dürrenmatt — $1.75
E345 **HEROES OF THE GREEKS** — Kerényi — $2.95
E347 **PSYCHOTHERAPY IN THE SOVIET UNION** — Winn — $1.95
E350 **THREE PLAYS** — Pinter — $1.95
E351 **THE ART OF MAKING DANCES** — Humphrey — $1.95
E353 **FRIGIDITY IN WOMEN, VOL. I** — Stekel — $1.95
E355 **PRESCRIPTION FOR REBELLION** — Lindner — $1.95
E356 **PSYCHOANALYSIS & CIVILIZATION** — Hollitscher — $1.45
E358 **INTRODUCTION TO MODERN EXISTENTIALISM** — Breisach — $2.45
E359 **THE LABYRINTH OF SOLITUDE** — Paz — $1.95
E360 **ZEN BUDDHISM & PSYCHOANALYSIS** — Suzuki, Fromm, DeMartino — $1.95
E364 **SELECTED POEMS OF PABLO NERUDA** — Belitt, trans. — $2.95
E365 **ARSHILE GORKY** — Rosenberg — $2.95

E368   **FICCIONES** — Borges — $2.45
E370   **EDUCATION FOR FREEDOM** — Hutchins — $1.45
E373   **HITLER'S SECRET BOOK** — $2.45
E374   **THE SCREENS** — Genet — $1.95
E375   **HELEN IN EGYPT** — H.D. — $2.45
E377   **MODERN GERMAN POETRY** — Hamburger, Middleton, eds. — $2.95
E378   **FILM: BOOK 2** — Hughes, ed. — $2.45
E379   **POEMS IN ENGLISH** — Beckett — $1.45
E380   **THE PHYSICISTS** — Dürrenmatt — $1.75
E381   **TOM JONES** — Osborne — $1.95
E382   **STAND UP, FRIEND, WITH ME** — Field — $1.45
E383   **TOWARD JAZZ** — Hodeir — $1.95
E384   **SYSTEMATIC SOCIOLOGY** — Mannheim — $1.75
E385   **TROPIC OF CAPRICORN** — Miller — $2.45
E386   **THE DEAD LECTURER** — LeRoi Jones — $1.45
E387   **NOTES & COUNTER NOTES** — Ionesco — $2.45
E388   **HOW IT IS** — Beckett — $1.95
E389   **WHAT IS EXISTENTIALISM?** — Barrett — $1.95
E390   **THE WRETCHED OF THE EARTH** — Fanon — $1.95
E391   **BERTHA AND OTHER PLAYS** — Koch — $1.95
E392   **THE ERASERS** — Robbe-Grillet — $1.95
E393   **ENTERTAINING MR. SLOANE** — Joe Orton — $1.45
E394   **SQUARE IN THE EYE** — Gelber — $1.95
E397   **THE STRUCTURE AND DYNAMICS OF ORGANIZATIONS AND GROUPS** — Berne — $2.45
E398   **SAN FRANCISCO AT YOUR FEET** — Doss — $1.95
E399   **INADMISSIBLE EVIDENCE** — Osborne — $1.75

If your bookseller doesn't have these books, you may order them by writing to Order Dept., Grove Press, Inc., 80 University Place, New York, New York 10003. Please enclose cash and add 25¢ for postage and handling.